A Consuming Fire

Eugene D. Genovese

A Consuming Fire

The Fall of the Confederacy
in the Mind of the
White Christian South

Mercer University Lamar Memorial Lectures, No. 41

THE UNIVERSITY OF GEORGIA PRESS

Athens & London

© 1998 by the University of Georgia Press
Athens, Georgia 30602
All rights reserved
Designed by Erin Kirk New
Set in 11 on 15 Bulmer by G & S Typesetters, Inc.
Printed and bound by Maple-Vail Book Manufacturing Group
The paper in this book meets the guidelines for
permanence and durability of the Committee on
Production Guidelines for Book Longevity of the
Council on Library Resources.

Printed in the United States of America
02 01 00 99   C 5 4 3 2

Library of Congress Cataloging in Publication Data
Genovese, Eugene D., 1930–
A consuming fire : the fall of the Confederacy in the mind of the
white Christian South / Eugene D. Genovese.
    p.   cm. — (Mercer University Lamar memorial lectures)
Includes bibliographical references (p.   ) and index.
ISBN 0-8203-2046-3 (alk. paper)
1. Slavery and the church—Southern States—History—19th
century.   2. Slavery—Southern States—History—19th century.
3. Southern States—History—1775–1865.   4. Southern
States—Church history—19th century.   5. Confederate States
of America—History—Religious aspects—Christianity.
I. Title.   II. Series.
E449.G3724 1998
261.8'34567'09750934—dc21   98-19482
                                                CIP

British Library Cataloging in Publication Data available

FOR DAVID MOLTKE-HANSEN

Take heed unto yourselves, lest ye forget the covenant of the Lord your God, which he made with you, and make you a graven image, or the likeness of any thing, which the Lord thy God hath forbidden thee.

. . . For the Lord thy God is a consuming fire, even a jealous God.

DEUTERONOMY 4:23–24

Contents

Foreword

Six years ago I took a graduate seminar on comparative slavery from one of the foremost living scholars of American history, Professor Eugene D. Genovese. Although I would enjoy engaging in a bit of revisionist history and say that I was not intimidated by his reputation, I cannot, for I was acutely aware that the man who sat at the head of the table had set the research agenda in the field. My anxiety was scarcely alleviated when he returned my first esssay to me. "This paper," his extensive comments began, "is, to say the least, infuriating." I am proud to say that I emerged from his seminar unscathed, ego somewhat intact, and undoubtedly a better historian. Over the years my appreciation of his talents as a scholar have grown immeasurably. Moreover, I have developed a deep fondness for Professor Genovese and I would like to think that I infuriate him less in my now wiser, more temperate days.

It was, perhaps, most fitting that Professor Genovese delivered the Forty-first Annual Lamar Memorial Lectures, "A Consuming Fire: The Fall of the Confederacy in the Mind of the White Christian South," from the podium of the Baptist minister Jesse Mercer, one of the University's founders. As Genovese notes, while the sectional crisis intensified during the 1850s, Southern divines argued that the South could defend the institution of slavery against attacks from the "infidel" abolitionists only by fulfilling their duties as Christian masters. The Lamar Committee thanks Professor Genovese for offering these challenging, provocative lectures. Our students were surely the beneficiaries of his committed interest in and engagement with the mind of the Southern slaveholding class. The committee also wishes to thank the family of the late Eugenia Blount Lamar, whose generous bequest makes this lecture series possible.

Personally I wish to thank John Shelton Reed, a former Lamar Lecturer, and Dale Reed for making the occasion of these Lamar Lectures exceedingly enjoyable. It is not often that the former landlords (and good friends) of the invited speaker are on hand, and I must note that Professor Reed trumped us all by delivering one of the wittiest introductions to a lecture in recent memory. I also wish to thank the members of the committee, each of whom did the difficult work long before I joined Mercer's faculty and the Lamar Committee: Mrs. R. Lanier Anderson III, Michael Cass, Fred Hobson, Hubert McAlexander, Wayne Mixon, Karen Orchard, George Tindall, and Henry Warnock.

Sarah E. Gardner
for the Lamar Memorial Lecture Committee

Preface

I am grateful to Professors Michael M. Cass and Sarah Gardner as well as their colleagues at Mercer University for having honored me with an invitation to deliver the Lamar Lectures. Together with their students and the good people of the Macon community, they favored me with formidable intellectual challenges to accompany their cheering warmth and exemplary hospitality.

I have rearranged the three lectures delivered at Mercer into four chapters. Where words appear in italics, the emphasis appeared in the texts quoted. Since the quotations contain so many errors or peculiarities of grammar, punctuation, and spelling, I have omitted *sic.*

Although this little book should speak for itself, some brief clarification may be in order. A focus on the religious dimension of the response to slavery, military defeat, and emancipation risks distortion, as all analytical isolation must, but it cannot be understood without attention to the political and economic exigencies of slaveholding. The proslavery divines of the Old South understood clearly, as did the more acute abolitionists, that the social relations of production—to invoke a Marxist category the slaveholders embraced without having read Marx—encouraged or retarded the spreading of the Gospel. Overwhelmingly, Southerners, even those who did not speak the language of "free will," agreed that everyone had to assume responsibility for his actions and inactions, but, in the eyes of the leading proslavery theorists, clerical and lay, social relations and material conditions affected the extent and pace of the spread of the Gospel and men's preparation to receive it. For proslavery spokesmen, "Christian slavery" offered the South—indeed, the world—the best hope for the vital work of preparation for the Kingdom, but they acknowledged that, from a Christian point of view, the slavery practiced in the South left much to be desired. For them, the struggle to reform or, rather, transform social relations was nothing less than a struggle to justify the trust God placed in them when He sanctioned slavery. This book explores the nature and consequences of their failure.

I have also returned to the old, hotly debated question of whether Southerners felt guilty about their ownership of slaves. Reviewing the work of those who have advanced the guilt thesis and rethinking my long-held opposition, I have concluded that we have all been excessively rigid in our formulation of the question and that a fresh look is needed.

I first became interested in the problem of the response to the fall of the Confederacy when, many years ago, I read Bell I. Wiley's essay, "The Movement to Humanize the Institution of Slavery During the Confederacy" (*Emory University Quarterly* 5 [1949]: 207–20). In *Roll, Jordan, Roll: The World the Slaves Made* (New York, 1974), I stressed the extent to which the reformers aimed to strengthen rather than undermine slavery. Believing that much more needed to be said, I continued to pursue the subject with growing attention to the depth of its religious dimension. Along the way, other scholars have treated some of the relevant themes in different contexts and offered fresh interpretations of their own, notably Drew Gilpin Faust in *The Creation of Confederate Nationalism: Ideology and Identity in the Civil War South* (Baton Rouge, La., 1988) and Mitchell Snay in *Gospel of Disunion: Religion and Separatism in the Antebellum South* (New York, 1993). I am deeply relieved when I agree with my learned colleagues, whose thoughtful evaluations of extensive primary materials command attention and respect. Where I disagree, the nature of the disagreements or, more likely, the different emphases will be readily apparent to those who have read these two books, as every serious student of Southern history must. Here, I wish to express my appreciation for Faust's and Snay's contributions and for the contributions of the many others—and, happily, there are now many— whose work on Southern religion is decisively reshaping our understanding of the slave society of the Old South.

I thank Amy Scott for doing heroic work in discovering the hiding places of obscure publications, for helping to check citations and footnotes, and for her Christian cheerfulness in putting up with my incurable grouchiness.

I cannot begin to express my indebtedness to the incomparably learned work of Jack Maddex—not only his articles on the religious dimension of the proslavery argument but the draft of portions of his forthcoming book on the Southern Presbyterians before and after the War, which promises to be a seminal work. In addition, Maddex offered painstaking criticism of the manuscript of *A Consuming Fire,* as did Robert Calhoon, Louis A. Ferleger, E. Brooks Holifield, David

Moltke-Hansen, Mark Noll, and Robert L. Paquette. Elizabeth
Fox-Genovese edited each draft of the manuscript with, if anything, more care and sweat than usual. She has always been my
toughest critic, and, in this case, she outdid herself.

So much for the amenities. What right my colleagues, to
say nothing of my wife, had to find errors and faults, I cannot imagine. But find them they did, thereby subjecting me
to acute embarrassment and the annoyance of having to make
substantial changes. From their long experience in the academic world, they doubtless know what to expect: much re-
sentment and little gratitude.

A Consuming Fire

CHAPTER ONE

Waiting on the Lord

The Lord is my light and my salvation; whom shall I fear? the Lord is the strength of my life; of whom shall I be afraid?

When the wicked, even mine enemies and my foes, came upon me to eat up my flesh, they stumbled and fell.

Though an host should encamp against me, my heart shall not fear: though war should rise against me, in this will I be confident.

Wait on the Lord: be of good courage, and he shall strengthen thine heart: wait, I say, on the Lord.

PSALMS 27:1–3, 14

In 1861 Southern Christians marched to war behind their Lord of Hosts, convinced that He blessed their struggle to uphold a scripturally sanctioned slavery and their right to national self-determination. The Episcopal Church in Virginia responded to the Yankee invasion by declaring the War "a Revolution, ecclesiastical as well as civil." The Methodist Reverend R. N. Sledd of Petersburg, Virginia, spoke for leading men in all denominations when he credited the South with fighting a religious war for the "cause of Christ, the interests of religion." Yet most of the leaders of all denominations had stood by the Union even through the turmoil of the 1850s, defecting only with Lincoln's election or even later with his call for troops.[1]

Virtually all Southern spokesmen, clerical and lay, readily acknowledged that the South was fighting to uphold slavery. When Bishop Stephen Elliott defined the stake as "the whole framework of our social life," he left no doubt that he considered slavery, state rights, and the other essentials of Southern doctrine as of a piece, and on this matter he, too, spoke for men in all denominations. Elliott moved into the secessionist camp early, but even those who held out to the last minute had been calling for a constitutional Union in which different social systems could coexist. As the Reverend J. S. Lamar of the

Christian Church put it: Northerners and Southerners differ "as radically and as rigidly as Puritanism differs from Christianity or as Abolitionism differs from the Bible."[2]

Southerners grounded the proslavery argument in an appeal to Scripture and denounced abolitionists as infidels who were abandoning the plain words of the Bible. The Southern divines, relying on the Word, forged a strong scriptural case. They cited the Old Testament to show that the Israelites, including Abraham and other favored patriarchs, held slaves without drawing God's censure. They cited the New Testament to demonstrate that neither Jesus nor the apostles ever preached against slavery and that, while Jesus drove the money changers from the temple, He never drove slaveholders from His church. Although most divines turned to the Noahic curse to provide a racial justification for the specific enslavement of blacks, the basic religious argument, abstractly considered, had nothing to do with race. The racial argument from Noah's curse was so feeble that James Henley Thornwell, Robert L. Dabney, and George Howe, the South's most formidable and influential theologians, rejected it as a rationale for slavery, and even the divines who espoused it gradually moved toward the social argument of the secular theorists. Together with George Fitzhugh, John Fletcher, James H. Hammond, George Frederick Holmes, and Henry Hughes, to mention only the most prominent secular theorists, the divines espoused personal servitude as the answer to the vexing "social question"—that is, the antagonistic relation of capital to labor.

Living in an era in which slavery had become racially specific, neither the divines nor the secular theorists were able to decouple "slavery in the abstract" from racial slavery, but they doggedly refused to accept race alone as an adequate justification for the social order. We shall consider the ramifications of their difficulty in chapter 3.[3]

Let us assume, *arguendo,* that the Bible does sanction slavery. As the proslavery divines and serious Christian laymen acknowledged, it also specifies the master-slave relation as a trust to be exercised in accordance with the Decalogue, the standards of the Abrahamic household, and the teachings of Jesus. The Southern divines had their work cut out for them, for they could hardly deny that Southern slavery, as legally constituted and daily practiced, fell well short of biblical standards. Accordingly, when they rallied their people to secession and war, they did not blithely assure them of a God-given victory. Instead, they warned that, to retain God's favor in a holy war, Southerners would have to prove worthy of His trust, specifically, of the trust He had placed in them as Christian masters. Hence, the divines called for repentance and reform.

Principal church leaders—Calvinist and Arminian, theologically orthodox and theologically liberal—agreed that God, in sanctioning slavery, commanded masters to follow the example of Abraham and to treat their slaves as members of their household and as brothers and sisters in the eyes of the Lord. Two questions haunted the sincere Christians among white Southerners: First, did not the actual conditions of slave life in the South significantly lapse from biblical standards? And second, would not the changes necessary to bring Southern slavery up to biblical standards in fact replace slavery with a markedly different form of personal servitude? These questions kept surfacing even in the texts of those who seemed chary of raising them directly. Prominent Catholics and Jews joined Protestants in upholding the biblical sanction for slavery while they complained that Southern slavery fell short of biblical norms.[4]

The preachers drew upon the lessons of Roman history to confirm the teachings of Scripture. The educators who shaped the minds of young Southerners invoked Cicero, Sallust, Tacitus, Horace, even Ovid to show that secular history reinforced sacred history. Augustine, to whom the Southern Calvinists were especially devoted, drew heavily on Sallust to argue that the vice and corruption of the Romans had provoked the wrath of God, who used barbarians to chastise them and finally to destroy their empire. Educated Southerners also knew a good deal about medieval history and had some favorite literary texts, notably *The Song of Roland*. As the Christian motives for Charlemagne's war in Spain got lost in assorted negotiations, compromises, and worldly considerations, God used the Saracens to bring down Roland and his comrades. And the reformers could turn to Edward Gibbon, another Southern favorite, who wrote of the Scythian conquest of Armenia in the eleventh century, "The Catholics were neither surprised nor displeased that a people so deeply infected with the Nestorian and Eutychian errors, had been delivered by Christ and his mother into the hands of infidels."[5]

The Southern jeremiads, which appealed to Scripture, history, and literature, had a long history. The early colonists imported slaves for work, not to Christianize and civilize poor, benighted Africans, and the majority never much exercised itself over pious injunctions to do their duty as Christians. Yet, from the start, a minority had seen Christianization as a solemn responsibility and never let the colonists forget their professions of philanthropy and innocence. During the second

quarter of the eighteenth century, Arthur Dibbs, Joseph Otten-
ghi, Noble Jones, William Stephens, George Whitefield, and
Samuel Davies, among others, accepted slavery as neither sinful nor necessarily impolitic, but they also insisted that it must
be brought up to standards of humanity described as scriptural
or Abrahamic or Christian. Whitefield, a hero to the planters
for his efforts to introduce slavery into Georgia, warned that
God had a quarrel with them for treating their slaves as brutes,
and Whitefield darkly suggested that the slaves would be morally justified if they rose in rebellion. Davies preached in Virginia during the mid-1750s with a strong emphasis on God's
stern punishment of those who did not repent of their sins.
Specifically, Davies invoked God's wrath against those who
were treating slaves inhumanely, and he referred to the setbacks suffered during the French and Indian War as evidence
of God's displeasure. When a cry for atonement for national
sins arose during the Revolutionary War, the sins in question
included slavery. Especially in the North, critics of slavery
specified not the treatment of slaves but slavery itself as the sin.
If Americans did not abolish slavery, they cried, God will un-
leash His wrath, and, among other consequences, America's
great republican experiment will fail. Southern slaveholders,
however, noticed that America did not abolish slavery, did win
its war, and did establish a stable republic. Whitefield, Davies,
and the men of the revolutionary generation did not accomplish their primary purpose, although they did prepare the way
for the nineteenth-century campaign to reform the slave codes.
As Bertram Wyatt-Brown has perceptively observed, Southern
preachers defended slavery as a positive good for the beneficial
uses to which genuinely Christian masters could put it.[6]

Early in the nineteenth century, in the wake of a protracted struggle over slavery within the churches, the Reverend Richard Furman of South Carolina took high ground in defense of slavery, and his *Views of the Baptists* had wide and deep repercussions in the South. The place and date of his open letter should be duly noted: Charleston, South Carolina, December 24, 1822. Furman was responding not so much to Denmark Vesey's attempt to raise a slave insurrection as to the reaction it provoked. Thus, even as Furman condemned the intended insurrection, he reserved his sternest reprimands for the harsh reprisals and the panicky demands for ever more repressive measures. The rebels had come out of the churches, rekindling old fears that religious instruction of the slaves would prove politically subversive. Furman had to defend the churches' commitment to the Christianization of the slaves and, simultaneously, to reassure slaveholders that the Bible, properly taught, would strengthen the social order. Whatever else he intended or effected, his open letter firmly called on Southerners to do their duty to their slaves, as a matter of both Christian conscience and political prudence.[7]

A quarter century later the Baptist Reverend Richard Fuller ably defended slavery in a widely read exchange of letters with the Reverend Francis Wayland, the antislavery Baptist president of Brown University, but, for such men as James H. Hammond, Fuller's defense of slavery left much to be desired. In the opening salvo in which Fuller denied the inherent sinfulness of slavery, he lamented the very existence of the slavery he was defending and fell back to historical ground. He pleaded that the British and the New Englanders had forced it upon the South, that Africans had long been enslaving each other, and that West Indian emancipation had failed and had engendered socioeconomic and moral decline, primarily because blacks would not work without compulsion.[8]

Now, if all this were true, why should Fuller have lamented the existence of slavery at all? The proslavery Wayne Gridley, among others, challenged him to explain why, under the circumstances Fuller had himself outlined, slavery should not continue indefinitely. Lamely, Fuller announced that he did not "abstractly" consider the perpetuation of slavery "proper, even if it be possible." Anticipating the question, why not, if it be no sin, he argued, "The Bible informs us what man is; and among such beings, irresponsible power is a trust too easily and too frequently abused." His reply might have led him to support emancipation, but he settled for amelioration. However timidly, Fuller joined those Southern divines who were calling for biblical standards and a sweeping revision of the slave codes.[9]

Until secession, reformers continued to preach the message crystallized by the Baptist Reverend Thornton Stringfellow of Virginia in the 1850s when he reminded the slaveholders that God had commanded the ancient Israelites to treat their slaves in accordance with His law. Stringfellow, like other Southerners, appealed to the same biblical texts to establish the legitimacy of slavery and to call for amelioration, for they saw the two appeals as integral parts of a single message. In proslavery sermons, preachers demanded obedience from slaves but no less forcefully demanded responsibility and restraint from masters. Former slaves testified that the same white preachers who kept annoying them with "obey your masters" sternly admonished masters to treat their slaves humanely in accordance with the Golden Rule.[10]

The clerical reformers slowly gained strength among the

laity. Increasingly, articles on good plantation management, written largely by slaveholders for each others' eyes and published in Southern agricultural journals, counseled the humane treatment of slaves as a matter of mutually reinforcing moral duty and material interest. Slaveholders constantly reminded each other that if they met their Christian responsibility to provide a comfortable life for their slaves, the reward would be good order and higher productivity. Prominent proslavery theorists who normally relied on secular argumentation— George Frederick Holmes, William Gilmore Simms, Nathaniel Beverley Tucker—also cited the Bible to warn that a wrathful God would punish Southerners who failed to live up to their ideals.[11]

With sectional tensions rising steadily, the wonder is that by the 1840s the campaign for reform persisted despite considerable self-censorship by reformers fearful of giving the abolitionists ammunition. The slaveholders had much to fear since the reform-minded Southern divines got nowhere when they appealed to the abolitionists for encouragement rather than denunciations. The immediatist abolitionists who emerged after 1831 issued a blanket condemnation of slavery as sinful and demanded emancipation without delay or compensation. They thereby denied that the slaveholders could or would reform themselves, and a free-market ideology led both abolitionists and Free-Soilers to view the proposed reforms as nothing short of a hypocrisy. They charged that the difference between the slavery that existed and that which was being projected constituted no difference at all, for any slavery remained an impermissible denial of freedom.[12]

The burgeoning abolitionist challenge bedeviled the efforts

of the reformers. Alexander Stephens sounded a perennial theme that reverberated among Southerners long after the War. Acknowledging that slavery stood in need of substantial reform, Stephens insisted that reformation had been slowly making headway and would have gone much further if the antislavery agitation had been put down. From the other end of the ideological spectrum, when James Gillespie Birney tried to launch an antislavery periodical in Kentucky, he encountered not only threats of mob action but also pleas from purported friends that antislavery agitation was only leading to worse conditions for blacks. The turmoil in Charleston in 1835 over the discovery of abolitionist literature at the post office could not have come at a worse time for the Episcopalians, who were about to issue a tract to promote the conversion of the blacks. Bishop Nathaniel Bowen charged that the abolitionist agitation was making it difficult, if not impossible, to press efforts to improve conditions.[13]

In 1840 the Reverend Robert L. Dabney worried that the abolitionist agitation was hardening the hearts of Virginians and thwarting efforts at reform. Dabney responded with a demand for higher standards. Specifically, blacks should not be executed for crimes for which whites were sentenced to a year or two in prison, and blacks must have the right to "resist wanton cruelty and injury." He excoriated "unprincipled" masters who inflicted starvation, oppression, and cruel punishments on their slaves. He urged protection of the family relation, noting that the black woman must be "mistress of her own chastity." If Southerners did not correct these abuses, he charged, they would be turning away from Jesus. In 1851, Dabney published a series of widely read articles in the *Richmond*

Enquirer and church publications in which he singled out the morality of slavery as the bedrock issue in the sectional quarrel. If Southerners stand firmly on the Bible, he wrote, the abolitionists will have to confess defeat or ruin themselves by exposing their infidelity. But, he added, Southerners can only stand on the Bible if they acknowledge that they have no right to separate man and wife or in any other way violate Christian teaching.[14]

Fuller, in his debate with Wayland, acknowledged that the slave laws generally needed considerable amendment but insisted that South Carolina would long ago have expunged its prohibition of slave literacy had it not been for the dangerous abolition agitation. Fuller had expected to advocate repeal in an address before the state agricultural society, but the president asked him to desist in view of the threat posed by incendiary publications: "I had, of course, to yield." Echoing Fuller, prominent reform-minded divines bowed to public opinion and defended oral instruction while they encouraged literate slaves to study the Bible. As John Girardeau told David Macrae, a touring Scotsman, after the War, he had wanted the slaves taught to read, but he had to acknowledge the dangers posed by abolitionist contamination. For Girardeau, as for others, the issue had always been touch and go.[15]

Abolitionist pressure took a heavy toll on those Southerners who were demanding reforms. In the 1840s jurists, led by the formidable John Belton O'Neall, the jewel of South Carolina's high court, criticized Southerners for allowing the abolitionists to bully them into repressive measures against slaves and free blacks. They appealed for amelioration as the politically safest as well as most Christian course. Yet even sober Southerners with antislavery tendencies, most notably George Tucker of Virginia, fell into apologetics. In the 1850s, Tucker, the South's and perhaps America's most accomplished political economist, complained that the abolition agitation had led to a worsening of conditions for the slaves. Thornwell, defending slavery before a huge Charleston congregation in 1850, prayed God to allow Southerners to maintain moderation and dignity in the face of abolitionist attacks: "It will be a signal proof that He has not condemned us, and a cheering token that in the vicissitudes of human affairs truth will ultimately prevail, and we shall stand acquitted at the bar of the world." [16]

During and after the 1830s, while state legislatures were steadily tightening the reins on slaves and free blacks alike, the demands for more humane treatment grew stronger despite cold indifference, stiff resistance, and endless claims of slave contentment under benign treatment. If nothing else, the agitation for reform revealed that slaveholders, prominent and obscure, were deeply troubled by the evidence of callous treatment. John Taylor of Caroline laid out the practical considerations early in the nineteenth century when he argued that the interests of the slaveholders as a class must prevail over individual interests. Thus, Taylor recommended more stringent laws to compel slaveholders to feed and clothe their slaves properly to discourage stealing.[17]

Preachers and Christian laymen acknowledged Taylor's argument from class interest, but they had even weightier considerations on their minds. By the early 1830s the religious press was protesting that the duties of masters to slaves needed closer consideration if widespread abuses were to be corrected and biblical standards upheld. Some divines concluded that amelioration would not work. Finis Ewing, one of the principal organizers of the Cumberland Presbyterian Church, freed his slaves and denounced the separation of families and the literacy laws, which forbade whites from teaching slaves to read and write. Ewing saw too many slaveholders who did not provide proper religious instruction or even clothe and feed their people properly.[18]

Few preachers followed Ewing into antislavery, but by the 1850s the great majority were pleading that the South could defend slavery only if it met its Christian responsibilities to the slaves. The South Carolina Methodist Conference dutifully denounced "the principles and opinions of the abolitionists *in toto*," but it simultaneously accused some slaveholders of mistreating their slaves by "excessive labor, extreme punishment, withholding necessary food and clothing, neglect in sickness or old age, and the like, and immoralities to be prevented or punished by all proper means." In 1850 the Reverend Ferdinand Jacobs of the Second Presbyterian Church of Charleston declared slavery a sacred trust but asked, "Is there no sin; no guilt of the blood of souls attached to us? Of any past indifference to this matter; of any neglect in regard to the highest interests of this relation, we should most earnestly repent, and from it reform, *if we expect God to accept us in the trust we would commit to him.*" The Episcopalian Bishop William Meade of Virginia, among others, sometimes made general pronouncements on national sins without specific mention of slavery but delivered other sermons in which he expressed concern over the treatment of slaves.[19]

Pleas not to give the abolitionists ammunition never stanched the demands for reform from within the ranks. In 1826 the governor of North Carolina told the legislature that the liberalization of the slave code would be proceeding apace were it not for abolitionist interference. In 1841, Kenneth Rayner repeated that claim in the U.S. House of Representatives. But in the 1850s, after decades of excuses, North Carolina became the terrain on which a powerful effort arose for a sweeping revision of the slave codes. In a proslavery tract widely circulated from the 1830s until the War, Chancellor William Harper of South Carolina called upon Southerners "to bear down even more strongly on masters who practise any wanton cruelty on their slaves." Harper elaborated, "The miscreant who is guilty of this not only violates the law of God and of humanity, but as far as in him lies, by bringing odium upon, endangers the institutions of his country, and the safety of his countrymen." Demands for the punishment of cruel masters grew apace among planters as well as clergymen and jurists, sometimes accompanied by heroic efforts of men who were ready to risk physical retaliation from those whom they accused. If nothing else, such efforts exposed an undercurrent of uneasiness into which reformers could tap.[20]

As prominent reform-minded clergymen recognized, they had to fight a two-front war among the slaveholders, first against professing Christians who took their responsibilities all too lightly, and second against those untroubled by Christian consciences. In 1841, Thornwell, after chatting with strangers on a stagecoach to Charleston, wrote to his wife that they opposed missions on the grounds that heathens were happy in their ignorance and would only be rendered discontented by receiving the Gospel. Thornwell suspected that his fellow passengers did not really believe that blacks had souls to save. Barely containing his rage, he condemned the "deplorable stupidity" of the "poor creatures," noting, "They never thought of their own salvation and how could they be expected to think of the salvation of others." As late as 1859, Charles Colcock Jones, with an eye on northwest Georgia, was complaining of the godlessness on the western frontier. He especially fretted about an irreligiousness that undermined respect for the slaves, and he called for a renewed and vigorous campaign for reform.[21]

The first problem the reformers had to face was among the easiest to solve. They had to convince masters to redouble efforts to bring their slaves to Christ. As the churches accommodated slavery, they gave high priority to those missions to the slaves which justified their theological and political position. During the great revival of 1829, for example, the Methodists proselytized blacks in earnest in a campaign that began most effectively in South Carolina and Georgia and quickly spread westward to Mississippi and northward to Virginia. The sectional split in the Baptist and Methodist churches in the mid-1840s generated an intensified effort to convert the slaves and a good deal of soul-searching among masters about the Christian nature of their relation to their slaves. Thus, the Cherokee Baptist Association of Texas, summing up the longstanding and commonly held view of almost all denominations in the South, hammered at the need for greater attention to the religious instruction of slaves. The association resolved in 1861, "Never were our obligations to God stronger with reference to this class of people than now. Slavery is an institution of divine appointment. To perpetuate it, we as Christians are pledged." It added, "The spiritual interest of this people we feel is committed in a great measure to our trust and our obligations we are bound sacredly to observe."[22]

Intensification of efforts at slave conversion accompanied demands for recognition of slave families at law and for repeal of the prohibitions against slave literacy. The churches had long cringed before the widespread criticism of the South's unwillingness to recognize slave marriages and prevent the separation of slave families. In proslavery theory, supported to some extent by the courts, marital and familial relations had at least minimal claims, and slaveholders, for practical as well as idealistic reasons, conceded the legitimacy of the slave family. The abolitionists nevertheless had a strong case: Without legal sanction, atrocities followed. Atrocities: not merely the injustices that necessarily befall all social relations in a sinful world.

From the beginning of the polemical wars over slavery the proslavery men had replied by comparing the condition of Southern slaves to that of laboring classes elsewhere. Among countless declarations, hear Robert Y. Hayne: "We have the consolation to know that our laboring population are in a condition greatly superior to that which they have occupied in their country or are perhaps destined to assume for ages to come, in any quarter of the globe." But even apologetics could be given a reformist twist, if with questionable effectiveness. The Reverend Joseph Cummings told the students of Emory and Henry College that the masses, free and slave, everywhere wallowed in ignorance, overworked and without time or energy to improve themselves. Southerners, he concluded, had a responsibility to see that the toil of their slaves did not become so relentless and oppressive that it would close them off from

the Christian message. Antislavery Northerners, both moderates and abolitionists, retorted sharply that Southern slavery
inherently contained outrages that vitiated all such compari-
sons. John Hersey, a moderate, replied that not even the most
despotic of kings in Europe would dare to claim the right to
break up families and sell husbands and wives, parents and
children, away from one another. The abolitionist Reverend
C. K. Whipple asked in 1858, "Do you know, Christian reader,
that no slave was ever prosecuted for bigamy or for fornication
or for adultery?"[23]

Few Southerners pretended that slave families were not broken up by sale or abused in other ways, although defenders of
slavery went to extraordinary lengths to minimize the extent of
such abuses. "We would not speak lightly of such an evil as
the destruction of family ties," wrote E. J. Pringle, who then
slipped into apologetics: "We deplore it as one of the hard
necessities of the poor man's position on earth." Pringle, along
with Louisa McCord and other proslavery writers, attacked the
exploitation of children and the separation of families in free-
labor countries, in which laborers fell victim to starvation.
They insisted that Southern slave families suffered less forced
separation than did families of the laboring classes of the North
or, indeed, of any country on earth subject to the vicissitudes
of economic necessity. As Pringle doubtless knew, the "you
are even worse than we are" argument may score well in po-
lemics, but it does nothing to ease Christian consciences. Julia
Tyler, George Sawyer, and no few others embellished Pringle's
claims, puffing that no respectable planter would break up a
slave family unless it were absolutely necessary. The abolitionists retorted that the commercial exigencies of the slave system

guaranteed a good deal of such economic pressure, even if countless slaveholders hated to yield to it. While insisting that conditions in the South were steadily improving, even Pringle admitted that the evil exists "as yet more than is necessary to the system."[24]

George D. Armstrong, a Presbyterian pastor in Norfolk, Virginia, inadvertently uttered a self-damning defense against the charge that his church never disciplined masters who separated families. Why, he knew of no members of his church who ever did such a thing. Armstrong was an honest man, so we may believe him. But his astonishing claim merely shed light on the unwillingness of many churchgoing Christians to become church members and submit to discipline. Dabney, as if to answer Armstrong, warned pastors to remember that they were more ignorant than anyone else about the "blemishes of the brethren" since the brethren were always unusually reserved in the presence of their pastors.[25]

As the apologetics continued, so did the grim insistence of the divines, jurists, and ordinary slaveholders on the urgency of reform. The Catholic Bishop Augustin Verot poured disgust on those who would make economic exigencies an excuse for their violation of the laws of God. The Presbyterian Reverend Charles Colcock Jones came down especially hard against the disruption of family ties. To render slavery orderly as a system, he maintained, the position of the father in the slave family had to be strengthened. The Reverend Robert J. Breckinridge of Kentucky, although himself a conservative emancipationist, spoke for many proslavery divines and jurists when he thundered that the violation of slave marriages made slavery "a hell upon earth." Thomas R. R. Cobb devoted much space in his widely read and highly praised *Inquiry into the Law of Negro Slavery* (1858) to criticism of the failure to protect slave marriages and the families at law. After the War, and much too late, John S. Wise, in *The End of an Era,* his fond portrait of life in old Virginia, described a slave auction and concluded that the mere sight of it should have told Southerners that slavery was wrong.[26]

Blacks raged against the separation of families more vigorously than they raged against any other feature of Southern slavery. John Brown, a fugitive slave from Georgia, replied tartly to Julia Tyler, "It is all very well for Mrs. Tyler to say that families are not often separated. I know better than that, and so does she." After the War, Mrs. H., who, as a slave, had beaten up a city official and lived to tell, told David Macrae that her masters had treated her kindly and that "there was good massas and good missuses." But she asked, "What was all dat if your chill'n could be sold from you, and you got to keep quiet?" Isaac Johnson had been a slave in Kentucky owned by his father, Richard Yeager, who had treated his mistress and her children well. One day Yeager saw a chance for a financial killing and sold his mistress and her three boys— separately. In later years Johnson cried out, "He had sold his own flesh and blood. That is what made American slavery possible. That is the 'Divine institution' we have heard so much about, the cornerstone of the proposed Confederacy." As free black men in Canada, John Martin and Daniel Hall reflected on their former masters. "Slavery is a dreadful thing," Martin remarked, "Slaveholders—I know not what will become of them. Some of them I love—but I know they deserve punishment, and leave them in the hands of God." Hall added, "I look at slavery as being heinous in the sight of God. And as for slaveholders, what is to become of people who take the husband from his wife, and the infant from his mother, and sell them where they can never see each other again?"[27]

In the words of H. W. Milburn, a Northern proslavery Methodist minister who spent six years in Alabama, "Such rendering asunder of the holiest bonds of our nature should not be allowed, cannot without incurring the dread anathema of a Christian civilization and the righteous indignation of God." On behalf of the Episcopalians and Roman Catholics, Bishops Elliott and Verot concurred and pleaded for a change in the law. Yet the Christian churches, which had long encouraged legal sanction of slave marriages and protection of families, did little to call parishioners to account. Church leaders relied on moral suasion and, in consequence, had much to be embarrassed about. Among other things, Southern Christians frequently hailed the moral superiority of their own faith relative to Islam, but they knew from their reading of Gibbon's *Decline and Fall of the Roman Empire* that Muhammed had forbidden Muslims to separate slave children from their mothers.[28]

In 1858, Christopher Memminger of South Carolina, a powerful politician who would sit in the Confederate cabinet, chaired a diocesan committee for the Episcopal Church to encourage measures to protect slave families from separation. Once again, the Church supported the principle that Christian masters should not separate families, and once again, it failed to take punitive action against those who transgressed. Bishop Elliott personally pleaded for the Church to request a change in state law, but the Church chose to avoid trouble and to rely on moral suasion. The Catholic Church, recognizing its fragile position in an evangelical Protestant South, usually took pains to avoid overt criticism of the regime, and, in any case, it, too, denied that slavery was inherently sinful. But bishops and priests, most notably the learned and prestigious Bishop John England of Charleston, felt compelled to speak out on slave marriages. In Missouri in 1844, Bishop Benedict J. Flaget threatened to excommunicate masters who refused to have their slaves receive the sacrament of marriage. Bishop Verot, calling for fundamental changes at law, declared that if Southerners proved unwilling to bring slavery up to biblical standards, they should expect God to "sweep Slavery out of the land, not because Slavery is bad in itself, but because men will abuse it through wanton malice." For good measure, Verot bravely demanded that "the rights of free persons of color be respected." [29]

The cause of reform made little headway in the legislatures before the War, but the steady drumbeat of its proponents was having an impact. When the Confederacy had to fight for its life and leading ministers were clamoring for the legalization of slave marriages, they touched raw nerves. In Nashville, Tennessee, John Berrien Lindsley, a prominent educator committed to slavery, Unionism, and white supremacy, asked in 1861 why God was chastising the South through the War. He answered, "Our divine Master has most emphatically ordained the family relations as sacred: The legislatures of the Southern States have with equal emphasis repudiated these relationships as to four million of their people. The Legislatures of each of these states has thus absolutely *nullified* the law of Christ. Can we wonder that they have been permitted in a fever of blind passion to overturn the government under which they had so highly prospered?" A year later Lindsley hoped that slavery would evolve into a more humane type of personal servitude.[30]

The literacy laws troubled the churches no less than the lack of legal status for slave marriages and family relations. Beginning in the eighteenth century church leaders chafed under the restrictions on slave literacy, especially those leaders troubled by slavery itself, not merely its abuses. As time went on, more and more influential religious leaders eschewed manumission and defended slavery, but they spoke sharply for amelioration until their voices reached a crescendo in the Confederacy. During the nineteenth century most Southern state legislatures declared unlawful the teaching of slaves to read and write, and the legislatures did so while public opinion was moving toward support of the campaign to Christianize the slaves. Most slaveholders, being Protestants wedded to the idea of private judgment, should have needed no sermons on the duty of every Christian to read the Bible for himself. The divines and the more seriously religious slaveholders squirmed.

The efforts to recognize slave marriage, to keep slave families intact, and to repeal the literacy laws confronted slaveholders with an uncomfortable choice between their religion and their political and socioeconomic interests. A widespread fear of black literacy gripped the slaveholders early despite assurances by Whitefield, Davies, and other formidable evangelists that the education of slaves would actually encourage good behavior. In 1828, Virginia Randolph Cary of Virginia caught the reformist temper in her book, *Letters on Female Character,* when she espoused literacy for the slaves as "a part of christian duty." Widespread doubts about black educability nonetheless reinforced the fear of dangerous political consequences. Albert Taylor Bledsoe, a principal political theorist and a once and future minister, doubted that slaves would profit from reading the Bible: "The tempter is not asleep. His eye is still, as ever of old, fixed on the forbidden tree; and thither he will point his hapless victims." Bledsoe would not consider a program for slave literacy while abolitionist incendiaries remained at large. But, in truth, he never seems to have believed that blacks were educable beyond the narrowest of limits, and after the War he derided black education as a waste of time and effort.[31]

Although the laws against teaching slaves to read and write proved difficult to enforce, slave illiteracy remained the norm, for it stemmed less from legislative prohibition than from the hostility or the indifference of masters. Hence, the evangelicals tried to make masters see the error of their ways. Churches in Kentucky set up schools for blacks and also enrolled them in Sabbath schools. But there as elsewhere by the 1830s public opinion made the education of black children increasingly difficult, not least because many recognized—and rejected—the manumissionist tendency of the proponents of literacy. Colonial Georgia had forbidden the teaching of slaves, but the new state government did not prohibit it until the aftermath of the Nat Turner rebellion and the onset of militant abolitionism in the 1830s. Then Georgia went the whole way and also made it an offense to provide slaves with paper or writing implements.[32]

Despite fears and doubts during the 1830s and 1840s, church leaders protested the literacy laws as an unpardonable denial of the Bible to black slaves whose souls were as precious as white in the sight of God. In 1838, in Abbeville, South

Carolina, for example, the Associate Reformed Presbyterian Church, supported by sixty-one slaveholders, petitioned for repeal of the obnoxious laws. Insisting that Christian slaveholders would ignore the literacy law anyway, opponents asked if the government intended to send spies into every slaveholding household.[33]

Throughout the South, churches and individuals quietly defied the proscription, and the bolder spirits campaigned against it. Some masters saw practical advantages to plantation management in having literate slaves; some masters, as Christians, had troubled consciences, whatever their fears. The Lucas family in the Carolina low country, including the celebrated Eliza Lucas Pinckney, spent much time in the education of their slave children, as did Samuel Davies, John Belton O'Neall, and others. According to Moses Stuart, when the elder Benjamin Morgan Palmer of Charleston, uncle of his more famous namesake, told Governor Hayne that he could not and would not obey the law against teaching slaves to read, Hayne replied, "Well, Doctor, we are not afraid that you will teach them anything bad. Do as you please, but keep it to yourself." The Catholic Church in Louisiana established schools for blacks early in the nineteenth century. In Missouri, which outlawed the teaching of slaves, numerous masters taught them privately. And in St. Louis the Catholic sisters, under the guise of teaching black girls to sew and knit, taught them to read. In short, despite the interposition of the law, a small but determined minority of slaveholders defiantly taught their slaves to read.[34]

In the 1840s, Charles Lyell reported that, in flagrant disregard of the law, "many" Virginians and some Georgians ignored the literacy law, and, tellingly, he also reported a thirst for knowledge among the slaves so favored. Especially embarrassing was the personal experience of some white Southerners with blacks who eagerly sought education and who outperformed the white children with whom they were taught. Notwithstanding brave efforts to teach blacks, community pressure against slave education in Texas, Florida, and South Carolina worked as well as legal prohibition. In late antebellum Alabama a Methodist preacher taught his slaves to read, only to have his neighbors threaten him with violence. According to O. J. M. McCann, an ex-slave, the preacher replied that "he would teach them to read the word of God if they hung him."[35]

The repression, at law or no, steadily deepened in the wake of slave revolts and plots. "An Old Citizen," writing in the *Georgetown Gazette* in 1799, questioned the good sense of his fellow South Carolinians who wanted to educate their slaves: "As soon as slaves are elevated they cease to be slaves, and will become masters at the first opportunity, as in St. Domingo." In speaking of slaves rather than blacks, Georgetown's "Old Citizen" was being no franker than most Southern commentators would be in later decades. The North Carolina legislative committee that recommended prohibition of slave literacy in the wake of the Nat Turner rebellion stressed the danger of subversion and insurrection, noting that a change for the worse had occurred in the attitude of slaves during the previous twenty years.[36]

Few if any argued that blacks lacked the capacity at least for elementary instruction, and those who did ran into endless taunts. Among many critics of slavery, Frances Kemble asked

why laws to forbid the education of slaves were necessary if
they were not bright enough to learn. During the War, when
Elizabeth Hyde Botume asked that question, she was told that,
of course, reference was to the "country niggers," for the town
slaves and house slaves, for that matter, "were smart enough
for anything." Slaveholders even defended the literacy laws
and the reliance upon oral instruction by praising the talent of
the blacks. N. G. North cited an illiterate black preacher who
knew the Bible by heart. Black children cannot read, "Tattler"
wrote in the *Southern Cultivator,* "but they know their cate-
chism as well as the white children who can read."[37]

Apologetics poured forth. Chancellor Harper wrote, "The
slave receives such instruction as qualifies him to discharge
the duties of his particular station." William S. Grayson of
Mississippi, citing reports that half the free population of England and two-thirds that of France were illiterate, concluded
dubiously, "It seems, then, that white laborers of England
and France are no better instructed than the black slaves of
America." Slaveholders defended the literacy laws by arguing
that the abolitionists were threatening to flood the South with
demagogic literature designed to foment rebellion among a
basically loyal and contented people who were nonetheless
simple-minded enough to be led astray. Especially after 1830
prominent divines as well as humble country preachers defended the literacy laws as a necessary evil and, biting their
lips, looked for ways to justify oral Christian instruction as a
viable option. Abolitionists responded that the slaveholders
were trying to convince themselves of their right to hold slave
property in perpetuity and knew that education would prepare
their slaves for freedom.[38]

White fears were hardly irrational. We need not believe the slaveholder who told Harriet Martineau that Southern slaves knew of Dr. Channing's antislavery book. But David Walker's famous pamphlet, which called the slaves to arms, did circulate among free blacks, North and South, and did reach some slaves, including some who could not read it for themselves. At that moment, some conservative participants in the constitutional debates in Virginia were warning that if gradual emancipation became state policy, slaves would not long tolerate their continued enslavement. In the 1840s Aaron Brown of Tennessee, in a congressional speech on the Gag Rule, maintained that enough slaves could read to guarantee their being aroused by a public campaign for abolition. In 1860 in North Carolina, Daniel Worth defended himself against an indictment for circulating Hinton Helper's *Impending Crisis of the South* by arguing that slaves, being illiterate, could not make use of it. The judge told him that, sooner or later, one way or another, all such messages would reach the slaves. Commenting from the bench on the literacy laws, Chief Justice Joseph Lumpkin of Georgia gave his "hearty and cordial approval" to the interdiction of everything calculated to render the slaves discontented.[39]

The arguments on both sides sometimes became tacky. In 1859, "A Mississippian" expressed a widespread sense of horror that Protestants could act like Roman Catholics in withholding the Bible from anyone: "If such a law is approved in a republican and Protestant community, it involves the absurd contradiction of professing a religious and political faith they will not practice, thus giving practical evidence of the truth and necessity of the Roman Catholic doctrine of absolute government in Church and State, that ignorance is the mother of devotion." This Mississippian and others like him were, in effect, answered in the 1830s by James H. Hammond, who turned the argument around and praised the Catholic Church for not making the mistake of trusting the Bible to the ignorant masses. Slaveholders in every state sorrowfully wished they could teach their slaves to read the Bible but pleaded that they could not take the risk.[40]

Yet the agitation for repeal of the obnoxious literacy laws continued, albeit with much backing and filling. The Reverend John Adger roared that no dangerous slave could be kept from subversive thoughts and actions by withholding the Bible from him. Such proscription merely kept the Word of God from good and morally inclined blacks. Charles Colcock Jones was not about to preach defiance of the law, which he acknowledged as a temporary political necessity, but he nonetheless denounced as enemies of God and man those slaveholders who kept the Bible from their slaves: "The Bible belongs of right to every man. It is the property of the world." Among jurists, John Belton O'Neall repeatedly insisted that he could not see how any Christian could withhold the Bible from another human being, and he taunted South Carolinians, who collectively referred to themselves as "the Chivalry," for appearing to fear their own slaves. Some influential editors supported him. Notably, in 1857 the Baptist Reverend N. M. Crawford of Penfield, South Carolina, son of William H. Crawford of Georgia, a leading presidential candidate in 1824, spoke out for repeal of the literacy laws.[41]

Other matters concerned the reformers, although none with the force of the conversion of the slaves, the sanctity of the

slave family, and the right of slaves to read the Bible. The almost forbidden matter of black testimony in court intruded
itself, if softly, and the admission of black testimony in church
trials proved bitterly divisive among Methodists in the early
1840s. Ignatius A. Few of Georgia infuriated antislavery Northern Methodists by insisting that the Church rule black testimony out of its courts in states that did not permit it at law.
Supporters of black testimony like Robert Y. Hayne and John
Belton O'Neall in South Carolina and Jefferson and Joseph
Davis in Mississippi denounced the prohibition of black testimony not only as an injustice to blacks but as subversive of the
law itself. White criminals, they protested, were going free in
cases when formidable evidence against them was being ruled
out of court, and juries had the intelligence to evaluate the
character of black witnesses and the credibility of their testimony. These objections did not get far. Resistance was, if anything, much stiffer than on other issues in a society that could
not bear the thought of convicting a white man on the word of
a black. Neither the Northern Methodist Reverend H. Mattison, who furiously attacked Few, nor the Southern reformers
invoked Deuteronomy 1:17, as they might well have: "Ye shall
not respect persons in judgment; but ye shall hear the small as
well as the great; ye shall not be afraid of the face of man; for
the judgment is God's."[42]

The vicissitudes of the movement for reform—the agitation, the timidity, the limits—emerged from the experience of
the Reverend H. N. McTyeire of Tennessee, scion of a South
Carolina planter family and a rising star in the Methodist
Church. In 1849 a Baptist State Convention offered a premium
of two hundred dollars for the best essay on the duties of

Christian masters, to be selected by an interdenominational committee, which awarded it to McTyeire. McTyeire's essay enjoyed wide circulation, and ten years later he brought out a book-length version, *Duties of Christian Masters.* Its principal themes, which had interdenominational endorsement, combined a scriptural defense of slavery with a forceful plea for biblical standards of slaveholding. Acknowledging many evils, McTyeire appealed for reforms in individual practice and cautiously suggested reforms at law. Yet he shied away from political demands and largely restricted himself to moral suasion.[43]

Notably, McTyeire called upon slaveholders to respect the marriage relation among their slaves, rendering it solemn through ritual, and to refuse to separate husband from wife. His argument strongly hinted at the need for recognition of slave marriages at law, but he did not confront the question directly. Similarly, he wrote that slaveholders condemned the "monstrous wrong and cruelty of tearing infant children away from parents, and putting asunder husband and wife," but he added the usual assurances that these atrocities occurred much more often in the free-labor countries of Europe. Again, he withheld demands for changes in the law, while he went out of his way to record the modest reform of the slave codes of Louisiana and Alabama, making it clear that he did not think they went far enough. McTyeire, clearly uncomfortable with the literacy laws, acknowledged the political necessity of preventing slaves from learning to read and proceeded to offer his own plan for oral instruction, "without entering at present upon the expediency or necessity of such a law." All in all, McTyeire laid bare what the reformers thought needful and what their communities resisted. The reformers themselves recognized the social danger of the reforms that the standards of divine righteousness required.

What, then, did the agitation for reform add up to before 1861? Politically and at law, not much. The legislatures took a few feeble steps to check vicious masters and insure minimal comfort for the slaves, and the courts, while jealously safeguarding the privileges, prerogatives, and profits of the masters, made an effort to provide judicial fairness to the slaves. The Pollyannas found just enough forward movement to take heart, and, while some of the more realistic became discouraged by the feeble results, others accepted the challenge to redouble their efforts. The principal gain lay in the impact on public opinion, which reflected considerable anxiety to repel the attacks of those abolitionists who ostensibly were responsible for the lack of substantial progress toward the Christianizing of the master-slave relation.

The mounting uneasiness sheds light on an old debate over whether many Southerners tormented themselves with guilt over their ownership of slaves. A good many able scholars have thought they did. In contrast, other scholars, myself included, have argued that the mass of the slaveholders—and nonslaveholders for that matter—accepted slavery as ubiquitous in history, as sanctioned by Scripture, and as a fact of life. But those who have advanced the guilt thesis have drawn attention to a problem that requires a fresh assessment. For if few slaveholders showed any guilt about their ownership of human beings, a great many confessed guilt over their inability to live according to their own professed standards of Christian slaveholding, and they worried about their ability to give a satisfactory account on Judgment Day of the stewardship upon which their own salvation depended. In 1861, Southerners found all their hopes, doubts, and fears, their complaints, theories, and proposals, crystallized in a war that put them on their mettle and put to the test their profession of submission to Christ.

Many Southerners had long viewed their struggle with the North with high hopes, others with foreboding, and some with both. Robert W. Barnwell of South Carolina fretted in 1845, "Our institutions are doomed, and the Southern civilization must go out in blood." James Anderson, a planter and Thornwell's son-in-law, wrote to a friend in 1858 that only an "inscrutable Providence" knew what would become of the South but that it would "doubtless be for his own glory." As the War began, the ministers, the great majority of whom were political moderates, pleaded that the Confederacy asked only to be left alone as a Christian country to serve the God whose help it now implored and in whose hands it thrust its fate. In the spirit of Psalm 27, pious Southerners waited on the Lord, trusting Him to act in His own way and in His good time. But as an old refrain runs, "Be careful what you pray for, lest you get it." As the South left the Union, Frederick Porcher, a firmly proslavery secessionist, spoke for many of his Southern brethren: "It may be that slavery is doomed. Be it so. Everything happens for the best. All that we ask is that it may perish manfully." [44]

We should not presume to know the mind of the Lord who proclaimed Himself "a consuming fire." We cannot know what prayers He chooses to favor or how He chooses to direct the affairs of men. But certain things we do know. The slaveholders did pray for a manly resolution. And they did go down in fire and blood.

CHAPTER TWO

Give an Account of Thy Stewardship

And he said also unto his disciples, There was a certain rich man, which had a steward; and the same was accused unto him that he had wasted his goods.

And he called him, and said unto him, How is it that I hear this of thee? give an account of thy stewardship; for thou mayest be no longer steward. . . .

He that is faithful in that which is least is faithful also in much: and he that is unjust in the least is unjust also in much.

LUKE 16:1 – 2, 10

All wars test the fiber of a nation, each war in a special way. In the War for Southern Independence the Confederacy had to prove itself a God-fearing nation in the eyes of the Lord of Hosts. As in every country and in every war, some Southern ministers, although fewer than often alleged, plunged into a chauvinism that verged on blasphemy, and a few actually preached that a just God could not possibly deny victory to the Confederacy. The Reverend William Harrison of Knoxville, to take one egregious example, announced that Jesus and His disciples were Southerners and Judas a Northerner. No wonder, then, that Rebecca Hunt Moulder, recalling her great-uncle, Thomas O'Connor of East Tennessee, wisecracked that during the spring and summer of 1857, "Knoxville church congregations were meeting to inform God where He stood in the prospect of disunion."[1]

The response of the divines did not depend on their theological orthodoxy or liberalism. The theologically liberal James Warley Miles wrote to his friend Mrs. Thomas John Young as the War began, "It would be impiety to doubt our triumph, because we are working out a great thought of God—namely the higher Development of Humanity in its capacity for Constitutional Liberty." And he added, "If our country accomplishes the destiny which God seems to have prepared for her, the bloody sacrifice will not have been too costly. Other

nations and other ages will reap fruits from the harvest we are
sowing." A typical layman's reaction came from John Esten
Cooke, Virginia's noted writer and an observant Episcopalian,
who declared at the death of Stonewall Jackson that God Al-
mighty would certainly deliver a Confederate victory.[2]

The early Confederate victories, most notably at Manassas,
inspired a spate of "God is with us" sermons. Preachers of
every denomination and in every state struck similar themes:
Manassas showed once again that right makes might; the
South was David, slaying the Philistine Goliath; God had intervened on the side of the Confederacy and sent His angel
to hurl back the Yankee invader; if God were not on the side
of the Confederacy, He would have crushed it already. The
preachers had to combat, even within themselves, the smug
notion that since the Confederacy had a just national cause, it
had nothing to confess or atone for. As late as 1863, the Presbyterian Reverend Drury Lacy cried out in an address at a
military hospital in North Carolina, "We are still *'a sinful
nation,' a people laden with iniquity, a seed of evil-doers, we
have provoked the Holy One of Israel to anger.*" And in 1864,
Thomas S. Dunaway of Virginia, a Baptist elder, reminded a
fast-day congregation, "We have not been invited, nor are we
here, to confess that we have trespassed or sinned against the
North, but against God, for it is against him, and him only, that
sin is committed."[3]

From the outset, preachers tried to rein in their elation and
speak prudently, avoiding the bad theology and dangerous
politics of those superpatriots who assured one and all that of
course God would deliver victory to His chosen Southern
people. In 1860, the Reverend William C. Dana of Charleston
spoke for much of the Southern clergy when he preached that,

notwithstanding the righteousness of the Southern cause, "the issues of things are with God." The Reverend C. S. Fedder bluntly told his congregation in Summerville, South Carolina, that God might choose to slay His sinful people and that they must be ready to submit to His will, whatever it might be. The Reverend John Leighton Wilson would say no more than that the early Confederate victories "may be regarded as an encouraging token of God's purpose to favor and bless our future Zion." Typically, even the more exuberant sermons offered no guarantees of a God-given victory, although congregants often had to listen carefully to register the caveats. Instead, the ministers stressed that God, not men and their armies, determined events and that the Confederacy must strive constantly to prove worthy of His favor.[4]

Among others, Bishop Atkinson of North Carolina and the Reverends William Butler of Virginia and J. S. Lamar of Georgia scoffed at the notion that God blesses all righteous causes. God, Atkinson chided, "does not always see fit to make right visibly triumphant." Butler asked how Southerners would cope with defeats if victories flowed from the nature of the cause rather than from God's blessing. With Confederate reverses at Roanoke Island, Nashville, and New Orleans, the preachers became steadily more sober. They pressed their message on the Confederacy's political leaders, especially when called upon to deliver sermons to the state legislatures. The Reverend S. H. Higgins told the Georgia General Assembly in 1863 that, while God intervenes in history to effect His own ends, His intervention does not necessarily signify His favor. Often, He uses a Nebuchadnezzar, an Alexander, a Caesar, a Napoleon to scourge sinful peoples.[5]

Even when the preachers got carried away by their own warlike rhetoric, they reminded their flock—and themselves—that war did not recommend itself as a Christian enterprise. Calvinists and Arminians shared a doctrine of salvation through grace that provided a powerful check on personal arrogance and national chauvinism. James Henley Thornwell set the tone in relentless attacks against national arrogance, most forcefully in his great "Sermon on National Sins," delivered in 1860 on a day of fasting and prayer for the salvation of the Union. He was speaking of all Americans, but his remarks retained their force when applied specifically to Southerners who were close to taking a political plunge that all too many were ready to claim as the will of God:

> I am far from believing that we alone, of all the people of the earth, are possessed of the true religion, and far from encouraging the narrow and exclusive spirit which, with the ancient hypocrites denounced by the Prophet, can complacently exclaim, The Temple of the Lord, the temple of the Lord, are we. Such arrogance and bigotry are utterly inconsistent with the penitential confessions which this day has been set apart to evoke. We are here, not like the Pharisee, to boast of our own righteousness, and to thank God that we are not like other men; but we are here like the poor publican, to smite upon our breasts, and to say, God be merciful to us sinners!

To be sure, Thornwell was calling upon Northerners to repent of their own sin in abandoning the Bible and denouncing slavery as sin, but, simultaneously, he was warning Southerners not to assume that because they were defending the Bible and its sanctification of slavery, they were proving themselves a people godly above all others.[6]

An impressive number of the Confederacy's religious leaders strove for balance, distinguishing just from unjust wars and denouncing wars of aggression as sins and crimes. In their more sober moments—alas, not all their moments were sober—they acknowledged that war demoralizes a people and disrupts the holy work of the churches. Even when steeling Confederate troops for battle, they tried not to get carried away. Thus, in Virginia in 1863, the Reverend J. J. D. Renfroe of Alabama justified the War but condemned the glorification of war itself as "a satire upon civilization, a legalized and scientific artifice for the destruction of human life on a mammoth scale."[7]

From the beginning of the War, church leaders like the Episcopalian bishops Thomas Atkinson, William Meade, and Richard Wilmer, while firmly supporting the Confederacy, acknowledged that war degrades and brutalizes its participants. They condemned the dehumanizing tendencies inherent in the most just of wars and the spirit of vengeance manifest on both sides. Meade characterized war as "the highest exhibition of hatred on the largest scale." The preachers admonished troops and civilians alike to conduct themselves in a civilized, Christian manner and to resist the temptation to hate their enemies. For the Baptists, the Reverend Sylvanus Landrum, among many, spoke in similar accents. Indeed, well before the War, John Leadley Dagg, the distinguished theologian and college president whose *Manual of Theology* was assigned in Baptist schools, referred to the failure of God's covenant with Israel as proof that war lies within our very nature and that we must constantly struggle against it through prayer. For the Methodists, the Reverend W. S. Doggett described war as a calamity

that arises not from God but from human passions. God uses
it to teach nations the errors of their ways and the folly of trying to settle issues with blood. Doggett added another thought
that conservative Southerners should have appreciated: War
breeds social disorder. Although God uses wars to chastise His
own favored but sinful people, the Presbyterian Reverend
Drury Lacy told wounded troops in 1863, war and fighting
stem from lust.[8]

The preaching went well beyond generalities about the nature of war. From the firing of the first shots, the preachers
excoriated the sin of pride as manifested in a swaggering chauvinism, in a distorted notion of chivalry, and in an excessive
cultivation of personal courage—all of which they condemned
as reliance on man and his armies instead of on God. In a related theme, Bishop Stephen Elliott and others stressed moral
over physical courage, defining the ultimate moral courage
as an unshakable faith in God and a willingness to submit to
His inscrutable will. The preachers harkened to the South's
long-standing attack on the free-labor North as a sewer of an
un-Christian radical individualism and a glorification of self.
They called, in the words the Reverend T. C. DeVeaux used in
1861, for prostration before God and for "renunciation of self-
dependence and self-reliance." The theme became more poi-
gnant by the beginning of 1865, when preachers like Charles
Minnigerode, rector of St. Paul's Church in Richmond, Virginia, desperately tried to shore up the hopes of a people who
knew that the Confederacy was falling.[9]

The preachers had trouble in juggling their thoughts to
strike the right balance. Bishop Alexander Gregg of Texas insisted that "War is not *evil* in itself " and that the religion of

Christ sanctions patriotism as a virtue. Yet in the same sermon Gregg described war as among the greatest of evils. Bishop Elliott branded war "as a great eater, a fierce, terrible, omnivorous eater" that destroys whole peoples and societies. Elliott cited the careers of Alexander, Caesar, and Napoleon to demonstrate that wars of conquest inexorably lead to further conquest, breeding corruption and ultimately destruction. But Elliott believed that great nations must pass through the test of war as part of a divine plan to perfect God's purposes. Elliott quoted Heraclitus, "War is the father of all things," to argue that prolonged peace wreaks its own toll, corrupting peoples and plunging them toward disasters. God, Elliott concluded, uses the chastisements of war to set His people back on the right course. The Reverend T. V. Moore of Richmond acknowledged war as "an evil, and often a sore and terrible evil, and a thing at variance with the spirit of the Gospel." Yet, no more than Elliott could Moore resist declaring, "War is not an unmitigated evil, terrible as its ravages are." For prolonged peace usually brings Mammon worship, corruption, effeminacy, and moral degeneracy with it. Thus, he concluded that God uses war to discipline His people.[10]

As the threat of war rose in 1860, Robert L. Dabney told the students at Hampden-Sydney College that God would punish those who became obsessed with making money and who indulged in the Southern penchant for dueling and the violent settling of personal scores. When the War came, Dabney impressed on Stonewall Jackson that Southerners might not prove up to God's challenge. Jackson agreed and told his troops that widespread sinfulness in the Confederacy posed a much greater threat than did the Union army. Robert E. Lee and numerous other military commanders repeatedly stressed that the Southern people would have to meet their Christian responsibilities if they expected God's continued favor. The preachers, meanwhile, continued to encourage confidence that God smiled on the Confederacy, primarily because they were interpreting the early Confederate victories as signs that the Confederacy was on His side.[11]

In 1862, Bishop James Otey of Tennessee spoke in Memphis on the indestructibility of the church in a world in which nations rose and fell: "Moral Earthquakes & political convulsions shake society, overturning thrones, destroying states & kingdoms, subverting the established order of things, rending it into fragments & sending through its deep fissures the pitchy smoke of fire—flood of burning passions & maiming prejudices, while [the church] calmly rises from her immovable foundations, a truth-palace, a world-refuge resplendent with beams of infinite love." Otey spoke as a strong Unionist who had gone with his state with the greatest reluctance, but Bishop Elliott, a militant secessionist, sounded the same alarm. The Confederacy, he said, was scoring brilliant successes, but it must expect reverses and even disasters during a trial in which it must show fortitude and prepare to accept God's will. Bishop Gregg declared that the cause of religion was "inseparably bound up" with the Confederate cause, but later in the War he rebutted the charge that the Episcopal Church had declared the Confederate struggle a holy crusade for godliness. Rather, he said, the South was defending its constitutional liberties against those who were threatening its religious life.[12]

In that spirit President Jefferson Davis, in his frequent fast-day pronouncements, invariably called for recognition that

Confederate victories were gifts of God that Southerners should acknowledge with humility, fear, and trembling. The principal form of "God is with us" had always contained the caveat that Southerners dare not alienate His affections by sinful behavior. The ministers presented in general the message for Southerners: The God who was on their side was testing them, and the outcome of the War depended upon their passing His tests, including His test of their rectitude as slaveholders.

While an impressive number of Confederate troops reiterated their faith in a cause they believed had God's blessing, they seem to have heeded the words of caution. Until the very end, surprisingly large numbers of Southerners refused to believe that God had abandoned their cause and remained convinced that He would deliver a last-minute victory against all odds. The War strengthened religion among the Confederate troops, producing what W. W. Bennett, a Southern Methodist leader, claimed as the greatest revival in world history. Especially in 1863, when Confederate prospects turned bleak, conversions soared, with a plausible estimate of 140,000.[13]

The preachers' success in bringing Confederate soldiers to Christ received a backhanded compliment from the Yankees, who cracked down hard on those they portrayed as the bulwarks of Southern resistance in occupied areas. Confederate General Edward Porter Alexander and William H. Trescot, a scholar and diplomat, offered backhanded compliments of their own. After the War, Alexander grumbled that there had been altogether too much praying. In his outstanding account of the War, he wrote acidly, "I think it was a serious incubus upon us that during the whole war our president & many of

our generals really and actually believed that there was this
mysterious Providence always hovering over the field & ready
to interfere on one side or the other, & that prayers & piety
might win its favor from day to day." Trescot wryly—and
unfairly—remarked, "Reverend priests, who had prayed fervently and prophesied boldly, placed their hands upon their
mouths and bowed in perplexed humility when they learned
that the ways of God were indeed past finding out."[14]

Confederate troops, despite an initial euphoria, did not long
rest complacently on their early victories. In the heady days of
1861, while scoring impressive victories, pious soldiers from
every part of the South made plain that they were ready to die,
secure in the knowledge that they were fighting for a cause
God would sustain. They easily thought, as William Maxey
of Georgia did, "We always will gain victory, for I believe
the Lord is on our side." Yet, while celebrating the triumphs
of 1861, Confederate troops remained sober. Hiram Camp of
Georgia wrote to his mother, "It looks like the Lord is on our
side, and I hope he will soon deliver us out of the trouble that
is now all over our Confederacy. Ma, I want your prayers and
pray that we may be able to live in the discharge of our duty
both as a Christian and a soldier. For the Bible says that
the prayers of the righteous availeth much." Before long, the
troops were in the forefront of those who were rallying to the
preachers' denunciations of godless behavior and proclaiming
the need to prove worthy of God's trust.[15]

The home front, much more readily than the front lines, felt
the preachers' wrath. Unrepentant sinfulness, they thundered,
threatened the great cause. The Methodist Reverend Augustus
Baldwin Longstreet, college president and author of the popu-

lar *Georgia Scenes*, thanked God that the South had finally seceded, but he warned that God would sustain the Confederacy only if Southerners changed their sinful ways. From different denominations, the Reverends Ferdinand Jacobs, J. S. Lamar, J. C. Mitchell, and Joel W. Tucker worried about the prevalence of sin but did not elaborate much beyond profanity and Sabbath-breaking. They preached in general terms that every Confederate victory signaled God's favor to His chosen people and every defeat His displeasure with their sins. The Baptist Reverend John Landing Burrows, among others, enumerated the sins: pride, drunkenness and high living, desecration of the Sabbath, blasphemy, greed, and a thirst for power and personal advancement. The Lutheran Church in South Carolina, in words that had their equivalent in the outbursts of other denominations, raged that "blasphemy, sabbath-breaking, selfishness, avarice, hardness of heart, unbelief, and many other evils abound." [16]

Throughout the War, the clergy and the press railed against the impiety, selfishness, corruption, and profiteering that threatened to bring God's wrath down on the Confederacy. In printed and widely circulated sermons, preachers denounced "extortion"—that is, price-gouging—with special frequency and ferocity. As the War dragged on, extortion, which preyed upon the poor and the helpless, became the sin most often specified as likely to incur God's wrath. Read aloud in army camps as well as in civilian family gatherings, the jeremiads spurred a harsh reaction especially among the troops. The Reverend William Wheelwright cried in 1862, "Self-seeking has cursed our cause for the past six months." Bishop Gregg denounced extortion as the worst sin to bedevil the Confederacy. The Reverend William Norwood raged, "*Avarice* is the crying sin in the land." Southerners' own "cupidity and extortion," the Methodist Reverend W. Rees agreed, is "worse than the foe." [17]

Confederate troops reacted furiously to the corruption behind the lines. Revealing their temper as well as anyone, William Stillwell, a Georgian at the front in Virginia, wrote to his wife in August 1863, "I am compelled to cry out, Oh, God, how long wilt Thou afflict us, how long will the horrors of war desolate our once happy country? Is the strength of God weakened or is his arm shortened? Nay, but the sins of the people have rose like a dark cloud between us and God, yes between us and the mercy seat." Stillwell elaborated, "We seek the creatures and not the creator. Speculators and extortioners seeking gain out of the blood of their brothers and women and children. I tell you, dear Mollie, unless the great God help us we are gone and how can we expect Him to bless such a people as we are? I once believed in the justice of our cause, but we have made it a curse and not a blessing. I believe that the next six months will decide our fate, and I fear it will be all against us. All that I can say is, God forbid." [18]

Trust in God went hand in hand with doubts about the people's gratitude for God's gifts and their readiness to repent of their sins. Albert H. Clark of Mississippi, a young Confederate officer on his way to Virginia, wrote, "Well, Bill, we can never be conquered only by the ruling power of God but alas! if God is against us, we are ruined forever." At the front in 1863, F. Stanley Russell wrote, "I trust that the God who has been with us so far in this struggle, may enable us to drive back the enemy at all points." But Russell asked the folks at home to pray more fervently, for he feared they were depending too much on the justice of the cause, "never thinking that it matters not how righteous the cause if we ourselves are not righteous how can we expect to succeed." Shortly thereafter, he declared all predictions useless since God alone would decide.[19]

Some soldiers focused their reactions more bitterly. The irate Barrier brothers, Rufas (or Rufus) and William, from a family of Unionist North Carolina planters, poured scorn on South Carolina and the South Carolinians. Both Barriers fought long and hard for the Confederacy—William sacrificed his life—but in letters to their father from the front, they identified the war profiteers with the radical secessionists, whom they charged, albeit without evidence, with being the very scoundrels who were getting rich by gouging the poor. "It would be pleasant to bleed and die in defence of our country," Rufas wrote, "if it were not for the thought of those vultures who are preying as it were upon our very vitals. . . . I think if there is a sin that is unpardonable, it is the sin of extortion."[20]

Through all the confusion and disappointments, and de-spite—or perhaps because of—the jeremiads, the preachers did a remarkable job of bolstering morale during the worst of times and holding out hopes of a Confederate victory. Virtually to the end, Walter Herron Taylor, Lee's adjutant, remained certain that God would deliver victory to the Confederacy, but he worried about the consequences of an insufficient piety in the ranks. In March 1863, he wrote to his wife, "But I fear not you, Bettie, God is your sure refuge, and you have only to cast all your hope on Him. I *too* wish that I could be again blessed with that peaceful, indescribable *spirit* which years ago I ex-perienced & which always seemed to bring me into close

proximity to my Saviour." Taylor feared not only that the War
might end badly but also that it was corrupting the Southern
people, who were inviting God's displeasure: "I am so hard-
ened; ah! sad indeed have been the effects of this unhappy
war—not the least of which has been the bitter spirit towards
our enemies which it has engendered, but which is entirely at
variance with the commands given for our guidance." Behind
the lines, those who, like Taylor, tried to suppress hatred for
the Yankees did not find it easy. Sarah Morgan rebuked herself
for hating the enemies whom Jesus commanded her to love,
but, as the Union army brought fire and sword to the South,
Eliza Frances Andrews could not bring herself to believe that
"when Christ said, 'Love your enemies,' he meant Yankees."
And each departure from the Word threatened doom. L. M.
DeSaussure hoped and prayed for the best but feared, "We are
not worthy, on acct. of our personal & national sins." After the
War, the Baptist Reverend J. Williams Jones simply concluded
that God had denied Southerners victory because too many
remained unconverted.[21]

The preachers called for repentance, and their parishioners
heard the message. John S. Palmer, a South Carolina planter,
wrote to his wife in July 1862, "War is the province of God and
must be meant to scourge nations for national sins. If so, then,
we must have incurred the finality and are now expiating in
full the calamities of the decree sent forth." In November 1865,
Samuel Matthews, formerly a minor state official, wrote to his
brother, Robert, from Panola, Mississippi, about the destruction of "churches, Masonic buildings, & school houses, corn
cribs, & gin houses, &c." and recalled, "God has often chastised nations for their sins, and often has chose the Heathen

round about to chastise his chosen people." Women of all
faiths spoke up in a similar manner. Pauline DeCaradeuc
Heyward, a Catholic, wrote in 1862, "I fear that our self-
confidence, boasting and pride of the successes accorded us
by God have weighed heavily in the balance against the justice of our cause in the hands of our Creator, and these reversals and terrible humiliations, come from Him to humble
our hearts and remind us of our total helplessness without His
aid." Kate Cumming, a wartime nurse, fretted that the sins
of the Confederacy must have been great indeed to provoke
such punishment. She did not mention slavery, and neither did
Ellen Beatty, Letitia Walton, Susan Cornwall, or Mary Jeffreys Bethell, although Bethell did reflect on the duty of white
Southerners to the freedmen. Bethell felt "like I am stript,
but is all for my good to make us seek rest and happiness in
God alone." The end of the War, she feared, had not ended
the woes and wickedness: "If the people don't repent I expect they will have some more judgements sent upon them, I
look for it." [22]

Increasingly, the list of sins to be repented of did include
slavery: not slavery per se, but its abuses. Reform-minded Confederates stepped up demands for the legalization of slave marriages and the protection of families against the sale of spouses
and children, for slave literacy, for severe punishment of cruel
masters, and even for admission of black testimony against
whites at law. These reformers made some little headway. In
Georgia the legislature repealed the law against the licensing
of black preachers and held masters responsible for providing
legal counsel for slaves accused of crimes. In Mississippi the
legislature apologetically turned aside proposals for reform,

but it allowed that they should receive consideration after the War. How much more could have been expected under the immediate circumstances? Despite the rage of the preachers, the churches themselves did not, as far as I know, expel those whom they branded as extortionists or amoral slave masters.

Yet a sense was growing that once the Confederacy won the War, it would have to open an intense debate over the condition of the slaves. In the summer and fall of 1861 the Episcopalian *Church Intelligencer* observed that secession had freed the South to attend to the reform of the slave codes, especially to protect the slave family, since it no longer had to worry about abolitionist interference. Indeed, in the eyes of ministers of all denominations, secession ended all excuses for foot-dragging. The Presbyterian Reverend Joseph Ruggles Wilson of Augusta, Georgia, spoke for much of the Southern clergy when, on January 1, 1861, he declared that an independent South could now vindicate slavery by curbing its abuses.[23]

Laymen, too, expressed the hope and expectation that secession would bring a new day in master-slave relations. In 1861 five judges in Richmond, Virginia, told Catherine Cooper Hopley that only Yankee mischief had kept Southerners from educating their slaves and that proper steps would follow a Confederate victory. Mary Jones of Georgia, widow of the Reverend Charles Colcock Jones, believed that Southerners treated their slaves better than slaveholders elsewhere did. But she admitted, "Not that we have done our duty to them here; far from it. I feel if ever we gain our independence there will be radical reforms in the system of slavery as it now exists. When once delivered from the interference of Northern abolitionism, we shall be free to make and enforce such rules and reformations as are just and right." The youthful Eliza Frances Andrews of Georgia suggested in 1865 that if the Confederacy won the War, it should enact legislation to confiscate the slaves of cruel masters and allow them to have masters of their own choice.[24]

In 1861 church leaders acknowledged, as the Reverend T. V. Moore gingerly put it, that slavery had its evils, which the abolitionist agitation had made it difficult to root out. Less gingerly, Bishop Meade ended a sermon at Millwood, Virginia: "Let us only see to it, that in our separation, when unmolested by misguided persons, who think of themselves, if not the only, yet the best friends of the African, we do our duty more faithfully to them in all respects." Less gingerly still, Bishop Elliott aggressively pursued the theme throughout the War in a manner designed to justify the South's commitment to "Christian slavery." In June 1861, he declared, "We are fighting to protect and preserve a race who form part of our household, and stand with us next to our children." And in September 1862, he said, "The great revolution through which we are passing certainly turns upon the point of slavery, and our future destiny is bound up with it. As we deal with it, so shall we prosper or suffer." If Southerners "assume the dominion of masters without remembering the duties thereof, God will 'make them pricks in our eyes and thorns in our sides, and shall vex us in the land wherein we dwell.'" In March 1863, Elliott praised the loyalty of the slaves and expressed hope that, after the War, the Confederacy would "render their domestic relations more permanent, and consult more closely their feelings and affections." In 1861, Bishop Augustin Verot, seconded by other Catholic bishops, published *A Tract for the Times,* in which

he demanded greater attention to the religious instruction of
slaves, stricter legal measures against those who did not provide adequately for their slaves, respect for slave marriages,
and an end to the sexual exploitation of female slaves. Slaveholders who ignored these duties, he added, were committing
"grievous sin." [25]

Military setbacks rendered the message all the more urgent.
In 1862, Bishop Gregg, who announced his belief in the "permanent inequality of the races," told an Episcopal convention
that revolutions, ecclesiastical and civil, rightly conducted,
permit the development of principles long dormant and present an opportunity to correct evils and errors. In November
1862, the Episcopalian bishops drafted a pastoral letter that
declared, "Not only our spiritual but our national life is
wrapped up in [the slaves'] welfare." Slaves, it warned, "are
not merely so much property, but are a sacred trust committed
to us, as a people, to be prepared for the work that God may
have for them to do, in the future." Acknowledging that the
Church included many of the South's biggest slaveholders, the
letter called for a redoubled effort to bring them to the highest
Christian standards. In particular, it attacked the separation of
slave families. The great work of reformation, it insisted, had
long been hindered by the circumstances created by the abolition agitation in the North, but now, with an independent
republic, Southerners had no excuse for delay.[26]

As the War progressed, more and more Southerners, even
when focusing on such evils as price-gouging, glumly concluded that God was punishing them for failing to meet their
full Christian responsibilities in evangelizing their slaves. Occasionally, with the wish father to the thought, preachers
claimed to see signs of a positive change in the attitude toward

the slaves. The Methodist Reverend I. R. Finley, preaching in Sussex County, Virginia, in 1863, expressed confidence that "the relations subsisting between master and slave are being placed upon a nobler and more stable basis, by the mutual discoveries of truth and duty." Regrettably, he offered no details. As time went on, preachers who had barely mentioned slavery began to do so. The Presbyterian Reverend Thomas Smyth became almost rapturous in his portrayals of God's use of heathens to discipline His chosen people in ancient times. In his *Soldier's Prayer Book* (1863), Smyth asked the Lord to make evident that He was indeed on the side of the Confederacy. Although Smyth called upon Southerners to repent of their sins, only once did he allude to the possibility that they were not meeting their obligations to the slaves. Subsequently, however, he reflected more deeply on the Confederacy's failure to uphold its responsibilities to the slaves, and he found in that failure the source of the military defeats.[27]

The divines preached the model of the Abrahamic household, and the jurists intoned about the human rights of servile laborers. Political exigencies had led them to minimize or dismiss the abolitionist indictments as falsehoods and gross exaggerations, but they privately admitted that the performance of their society fell far short of its professed standards. Slowly but steadily, the calls for repentance focused on sins associated with slavery. In Texas, Mary Watkins wrote to her mother back in Mississippi, "As I heard our minister say a short time ago, 'slavery is right if used righteously, otherwise it is not.'" In Georgia, Dolly Burge, a pious plantation mistress who did not doubt the biblical sanction for slavery, nonetheless confessed misgivings simply because too many slaveholders abused their power.[28]

In Natchez, Mississippi, the proslavery and militantly racist Dr. William Henry Holcombe had similar misgivings. He regretted the intellectual indolence bred by slavery and the consequent willingness of many clergymen and statesmen to tolerate its undeniable evils. Tellingly, even those who focused on corruption and extortion as the Confederacy's greatest sins began to espy a connection with the sins associated with slavery or to fear that God would punish the slaveholders by taking away their slaves. The Reverend W. Cave of Tallahassee, Florida, specified the connection when he denounced planters for the rampant love of money that led them to drive their slaves impermissibly. R. C. Saffold of Mississippi wrote to Governor John Pettus, "Sometimes I am almost given to think that the slaveholder is a doomed man, especially when he closes his corn house against the hungry. Quem Deus Vult." Benjamin F. Perry of South Carolina denounced the speculators for endangering slavery: "God will punish them in some way & I fear it is by the emancipation of their slaves!"[29]

The reformers proceeded against great odds, for the sharpening focus on the treatment of slaves by white Christians was by no means always welcome. By 1863, when the religious press was attributing military reverses to God's anger at the failure to attend to the needs of the slaves, the reformers frankly admitted that they were still working in a hostile atmosphere in which, as a writer in the *Southern Presbyterian Review* delicately put it, "the abuses incident to the relation, and the remedies for them, if not virtually tabooed amongst us, have been at least subordinated to other more menacing aspects of the angry controversy."[30]

As the war news grew worse, preachers in every denomination and in every part of the South intensified their warning: Slaveholders must not provoke the God of Wrath by continuing to fall short as masters. Georgia's Methodists had long been hearing demands for reform of the slave codes from Bishop George Foster Pierce, among others, and the Church Conference responded during the War by petitioning the state legislature to protect slave families. Baptist preachers combined a celebration of the Confederate cause as God's own with prophesies of calamity if Southerners did not confess and repent of their sins. In Richmond, the Roman Catholic Bishop John McGill described the War as "a scourge of God" on the slaveholders for failing to sanction slave marriages and protect slave families.[31]

In 1863, Calvin H. Wiley of North Carolina presented a comprehensive case for reform in his book, *Scriptural Views of National Trials*. A devout Presbyterian who became a minister after the War, Wiley's stature and influence may be measured by his having been warmly praised and supported by both Whigs and Democrats for his great work for public education during the 1850s. He endorsed all the principal proposals for reform and asserted that the fate of the Confederacy depended on their enactment. If the slaveholders did not repent of their sins and render full justice to the slaves in their charge, they would be crushed by an angry God. Wiley reviewed biblical history to show that God often uses heathens, like the Yankees, to humble His chosen people when they go astray. Wiley forcefully refuted those facile preachers who were saying that since the war pitted Christian Southerners against infidel Yankees, Confederate victory was assured. Wiley sought to strengthen slavery by reforming it at law in accordance with scriptural prescription. Even the trials of the War did not weaken his commitment, and he strongly opposed as dangerously subversive the plan to recruit black troops for the Confederacy.[32]

For the Baptists, the influential Reverend Isaac Taylor Tichenor, addressing the General Assembly of Alabama in 1863, expressed confidence that God would vindicate the Confederacy, but he warned that the continued abuses of slavery lay at the root of military reversals. "We have failed to discharge our duties to our slaves," he protested, adding, "Marriage is a divine institution, and yet marriage exists among our slaves dependent upon the will of the master. 'What God has joined together, let no man put asunder,' yet this tie is subject to the passion, caprice or avarice of their owners." Tichenor expressed confidence that God was preparing the South to show the world the superiority of slavery as a social system that reconciled the interests of labor and capital. But to enjoy God's favor, Southerners must demonstrate "a proper understanding and regard for the rights of both master and servant."[33]

Preaching to the legislatures of South Carolina and Georgia in 1863, the Methodist Bishop Pierce also exuded confidence in the victory of the slaveholding Confederacy, while he cautioned that Southerners must first repent of their sins. Pierce launched a ferocious attack on the literacy laws. If, he taunted, the Bible sanctions slavery, then slaveholders should want a Bible in every slave cabin in the South. Why, in any case, should Southerners make the blacks suffer for the sins of the Yankees? The periodicals of the several denominations echoed the sentiment. The churches stepped up pressure to petition state legislatures to repeal the literacy laws, and they gathered support from ardent proslavery laymen like J. A. Turner, the much respected editor of the *Countryman* in up-country Georgia.[34]

In the Southwest, the Reverend James A. Lyon of Colum-bus, Mississippi, emerged as the principal spokesman for the reformers. Lyon, an antisecessionist, boldly spoke up for an overhauling of the slave codes as soon as the War began. In 1863 he chaired a select committee of the Presbyterian Church to consider the proper role of the Church in such matters. Lyon's draft made clear his support for slavery, or at least for some kind of servitude: "As to the lawfulness of the institution slavery in itself considered, disconnected from its abuses, we scarcely deem it necessary to discuss it. Like the existence of God, it is taken for granted from the beginning to the end of the Bible." Slavery, the report continued, "has existed in all past ages, and will continue to exist for ages yet to come. It is incidental to a state of sin and depravity. . . . It will continue to be necessary, until Christianity gain such ascendancy over the minds and hearts and lives of men—all men—as to bring the entire race under the absolute and delightful control of the principles of the Gospel. Then slavery will, as a natural result, cease." Meanwhile, Southerners should recognize that slavery would be inexcusable in God's eyes were it not conducted in a manner just and equitable.[35]

The report bristled at the refusal of Protestants to teach any Christians to read the Bible and asserted that the more the intelligence of a slave was developed, the more useful and con-tented he would become. It proposed repeal of the literacy laws, although it opposed the establishment of schools for slaves, arguing that masters themselves should assume direct

responsibility. It insisted that the literacy laws were a "dead
letter" anyway, since masters who wished to evade them already did so. Safely enough, the report attacked absenteeism
and demanded that masters give their slaves personal attention.
More boldly, it called for the admission of slave testimony in
court, subject to extreme discretion in evaluating it. The exclu-
sion of slave testimony, it said, had been justified while African
slaves were savages, but not now, when they were enlightened
by Christianity. Above all, the report demanded that the law
recognize and protect slave marriages: "There is nothing in
our legislation, so far as we know, that recognizes marriage
between the slaves; or prohibits fornication, adultery, bigamy,
incest, or even rape amongst them. This is an outrage upon
the laws of God, both natural and revealed, except on the pre-
sumption that the slave is not a man, but a *brute*, with a brute's
propensities, a brute's nature, and a brute's destiny."

The report stressed that the establishment of the Confederacy removed the danger of abolitionist tampering with slaves
and, with it, all excuse for further delay in the urgently needed
reform. With a bow to Noah's curse, it suggested that since
"Ethiopia will stretch out her hands unto God," white Southerners had a duty to live up to God's trust by doing everything
in their power to elevate the black race. And the report warned
that if whites did not do so, God would smite them. In the
end, the Church, responding to political exigencies, hesitated
to press its demands. But the agitation got the attention of the
governor and legislators, who acknowledged that the matter
would have to be dealt with after the War.[36]

The divines' wartime proposals differed little, if at all, from
those they and others had advanced before secession, and it is

difficult to see how they could have proceeded differently. To propose anything less would have fallen woefully short of Christian teaching; to propose anything more would have threatened a transformation of chattel slavery into an alternate form of bound labor and, hence, the abolition of slavery itself. The distinctive character of the wartime proposals lay in the recognition that reform now lay within the slaveholders' power. The time to live up to professed convictions had arrived.

Pleas for reform, like much else, had to proceed amid a deepening crisis of faith, which took root even before Appomattox. As the Union armies advanced, doubts about God's justice and goodness threatened to shatter the land. Robert L. Dabney summed up the increasingly desperate plight of the Confederacy in a memorial sermon on Lieutenant Colonel John T. Thornton. He called for submission to God's will and simultaneously reiterated his confidence in a Confederate victory: "In thine own appointed time, Oh God, thou wilt deliver us from the hands of our enemies and of those who hate us." In 1863, Dabney preached a memorial sermon on the death of Stonewall Jackson, whom he had served as a military aide and whom he regarded as an exemplar of Christian courage. Dabney warned that the child of God does not pretend to have a guarantee of personal security. And he added pointedly, "Nor does he presume to predict what particular dispensation God will grant to the cause in which he is embarked."[37]

In the dark days of 1864, the Presbyterian Reverend William T. Hall declared that a Confederate defeat would be "the only inexplicable anomaly of history." From the beginning of the War, some preachers, like Joel W. Tucker of Fayetteville, North Carolina, virtually declared the ultimate failure of the

Confederacy to be an impossibility even while warning that
God was testing His people. Hall was speaking carelessly—
something unusual for this deeply thoughtful, scholarly man—
and he was taking a dangerous tack. By reiterating his faith in
delivery by the Lord of Hosts, he was inviting disillusionment
if the War should end badly. Thus Paul Hayne, the celebrated
poet, never could understand how God had allowed the Yankees to conquer the South. As late as 1885 he confessed to his
wife, it is "the puzzle of puzzles," adding, "My very *faith* is
sometimes shaken by it, & I think of Napoleon's or some Con-
queror's aphorism about 'Providence being always on the side
of the *heaviest artillery.*'" [38]

Even women, ostensibly superior to men in piety, struggled
to maintain their faith as the Yankees rolled through their beloved South. "It is terrible to have our once happy homes so
devastated," Sally Kollock of North Carolina said, "and if there
were not a righteous God who rules us, I should sometimes
almost despair." But she remained hopeful that "after we have
been purified by suffering, God will deliver us from our enemies." As early as 1862 in Mississippi, a despondent Sarah
Watkins wrote to her daughter, "We are almost whipped. I put
my trust in God, his will must be done. If the South is sub-
dued it is the will of the Lord for it to be done and we must
be resigned to his will and trust in him to take care of us."
The young Sarah Lois Wadley could not so readily deny her
doubts. Feeling the effects of Confederate reversals in 1863, she
reiterated her belief that God controlled all events, and she
vowed to yield to His will. But she was having a hard time:
"Surely he will deliver us and, if not, if it be his will to take
from us what is dearer than home, friends, or life itself, our

country, can I not believe that Our Father doeth all things well. I will try thus to believe, Oh Lord, help thou mine unbelief." Grace Elmore, a novelist, confessed that the defeat of the Confederacy rendered her so distraught that she contemplated suicide.[39]

Defeat and its aftermath led some Southerners to speculate about the role of Satan. When the denominational press debated the religious significance of emancipation, some suggested that since God could not possibly have freed the slaves from a social arrangement that He had ordained for the good of all, the Devil was having one of his temporary moments of triumph. Nannie Eiland Lewis of Alabama, a conscientious Presbyterian, wrote to her niece in 1866 that she had experienced "a world of troubles" since they had last met: "I know the Lord is gracious and slow to anger and plentious in mercy. Dear Mollie if I could only acknowledge God's hand in all that this terrible war has inflicted upon me it would be a great consolation, but when I see so much vice and wickedness I cannot help thinking saten [Satan] is set loose." A despairing Elizabeth Hardin risked the deepest of sins when, for a moment at least, she hoped to turn Satan into an ally: She would be "tempted to cry 'Vive Beelzebub' if he were fighting the Yankees." The Reverend Jesse Cox of Tennessee saw fulfillment of biblical prophecy with the Yankee invaders as the Antichrist, the Beast of Revelation, but in 1863, as the tide turned against the Confederacy, Cox recovered and proclaimed his total dependence on the Lord.[40]

The fall of the Confederacy proved traumatic for the white Christians of the South. As the preachers and church journals acknowledged, in the excruciating struggle to affirm faith in

God's goodness and justice, some Southerners, at least momentarily, doubted the existence of God. Still, however many men returned from the War with broken spirits, many others, like William Peagram and David Wesley Martin, returned with renewed trust in God's inscrutable will. In 1865, Susan Caldwell of Warrenton, Virginia, wrote to her father that the Yankees were coming and she could not take much more grief: "I am tired of living such a life—but oh! why should I complain when thousands are faring worse than I—God help me to be resigned. I long to be a true pious christian—to live for Heaven—to feel assured I shall reach there—to be at rest—but I find it hard. My heart is so *Rebellious.*" Some men and women never did recover, but most did, if in different ways. With the War lost, W. P. Chambers wrote, "It is a sweet sentence which says, 'God loveth whom he chasteneth.' No worldly prosperity and no national success should make us for one moment willing to forego the love of the eternal Father." In January 1865, he acknowledged, "It may be that God deigns our overthrow as a separate government. If so, may He prepare us for the ordeal that awaits us as a conquered people. There is too much iniquity in the land, in high places and low too, for us to expect any interposition of providence in our behalf. May He teach us our duty." [41]

Josiah Gorgas, the Confederacy's outstanding ordnance officer, remained convinced of victory until the last moment. Defeat shook him: "Providence seems to have utterly abandoned us to our enemies, and we have nothing to do but submit." On July 1, 1866, Gorgas recalled that he had expected trials and disappointments but "believed in the goodness of our cause" and its triumph. "Alas, it has failed & leaves my life as to its future bitter and barren. I cannot believe that there is no future for this country but abject submission to the puritan." John S. Wise taunted the Yankees, "After all, it was not you, but God that abolished slavery. You were his mere instruments to do his work." Although a terrific one-liner, Wise's statement probably did little to relieve the pain.[42]

As if to reply to Gorgas and the many like him, the Presbyterian Reverend Dr. William Brown exhorted in 1865, "You have been called upon to pass through deep waters; you have had sorrow upon sorrow. It was the path your Savior trod and He will grant you in it the comfort of His love and the fellowship of His Spirit." Brown pleaded, "Remember, that the church of God has often passed through the heated furnace, but the form of the Son of God has been seen with her and she is still unconsumed."[43]

Distraught ministers had to deliver such sermons to themselves and to each other as they writhed with doubts they never thought they would experience. Shaler Granby Hillyer, a prominent Baptist minister and professor of theology at Mercer University, lost his son during the War. The devastated Hillyer's faith was shaken, only to be revived by the preaching of a fellow Baptist minister. The secessionist Reverend C. P. Gadsden, rector of St. Luke's Episcopal Church in Charleston, resigned himself to the crushing of his earthly hopes and reaffirmed his trust in God, resuming his pastoral work with undiminished zeal and patience. The Reverend Washington Manly Wingate, president of Wake Forest College, one of the greatest Baptist preachers in North Carolina, and an ardent Confederate partisan, found himself in rebellion against God upon hearing of Lee's surrender. He locked himself in his parlor and struggled with himself and his God, emerging repentant and submissive. He then preached what his admirers thought one of his greatest sermons, "And we know that all things work together for good to them who love God, to them who are called according to his purpose."[44]

Slowly and bitterly, Southerners came to rue the confusion of a patriotic military struggle presumably waged with God's grace and the struggle for the salvation of their immortal souls. And confusion there was, as some preachers, wishing to console the bereaved, slipped into the blasphemy of speaking of the Confederate dead as martyrs for Christ. Frances Brokenbrough, in her widely circulated *A Mother's Parting Words to Her Soldier Boy,* issued a sharp rebuke to the errant: "I gave up my son, without reluctance, indeed I may say with joy, to enter the army of his country. The war in which we are unfortunately involved, has been forced upon us. We have asked for nothing but to be let alone. We are contending for the great fundamental principle of the American Revolution: that all authority is derived from the consent of the governed." But, she added pointedly, "Christ did not promise eternal life to those who fell in battle for their country but to those who triumphed over sin." Patriotism, she insisted, is no substitute for piety: "The heroic but ungodly soldier may fill a grave honored by his nation's tears and marked by a towering monument, but his soul, alas! must perish." Ellen House rebuked herself for sinning when she repined over the desolation caused by the War. When the end came, this fiery rebel moaned, "We have depended too much on Gen. Lee too little on God." She prayed fervently to accept God's will, and she chastised herself for not being able to overcome her hatred for the Yankees. As she reminded herself, patriotism will not save the soul.[45]

The Southern Jeremiahs lived to say, "I told you so." They had, after all, long warned against a misreading of the signs of the times. With the fall of the Confederacy, Bishop Verot bluntly attributed the defeat to the slaveholders' failure to treat their slaves in accordance with scriptural injunction. Lyon mused, "Perhaps God's intentions are to bring the institution [of slavery] to an absolute end." In the 1870s, John Girardeau, John Adger, and Benjamin Morgan Palmer, all leading Presbyterian divines, softened but did not challenge that message. "The Southern church," they declared, "makes no boast that she did her whole duty to the souls of the slaves. As before God, she has much to confess; but as before men, she can honestly affirm that she did not neglect the spiritual interests of the Negro, but sincerely endeavored to lead him to Christ."[46]

John Leadley Dagg had warned in 1857, in his widely read *Manual of Theology,* that the Israelites, God's chosen people, had done nothing to earn His favor. God chose them for His own reasons and, when they violated His covenant, He punished them severely. During the War Dagg described Southern afflictions not as "tokens of perdition" but as "fatherly chastisements, designed for our profit." He feared that Southerners were misusing the institution God had entrusted to them: "The failure of our laws to recognize and protect marriage among slaves has attracted the attention of our religious bodies, but this failure is only a part of the general evil. We have not labored, in every possible way, to promote the welfare, for time and eternity, of our slave population, as of dependent and helpless immortals whom God has placed in our power and at our mercy." To avoid the impending catastrophe, Southerners had to change course abruptly. In 1866 Dagg returned to the theme. God inflicted defeat upon the Confederacy, he wrote, because its people failed in their duty to their black dependents, who needed white protection now more than ever. White Southerners dared not fail them again.[47]

Laymen reacted similarly. In the throes of defeat in 1865, Bishop Thomas Atkinson, addressing his Episcopalian flock in North Carolina, referred to the widespread feeling that, despite much good effort, masters had simply not done their full duty to their slaves. George Flournoy, a former Texas attorney general who fled to Mexico at the end of the War, concluded that God had cursed slavery in the wake of the Southerners' failure to improve the moral and material condition of the slaves. After the War women published memoirs and novels in which they clung to the notion that God was punishing Southerners for their sins—not for having been slaveholders but for failing in their duty as masters. Henry William Ravenel, an eminent botanist and pious Episcopalian, surveying the ruins in 1865, gloomily admitted that slaveholders had erred in failing to reform the slave codes in time. He especially regretted the failure to protect slave marriages and families. "Perhaps," he mused, "it is for neglecting these obligations that God has seen fit to dissolve that relation." He prayed that emancipation would benefit the slaves, and he did his best for them. A Unionist and then a cooperationist-secessionist, Ravenel had long upheld the proslavery cause, but he concluded that God had declared against it: "I accept the issue from His hands—

& am content. . . . I submit without discontent because I know that infinite wisdom cannot err."[48]

When the War was all but lost, throngs filled the streets of Charleston, fervently praying for a Confederate victory. "In consequence of its disastrous result," John Girardeau wrote, "many of God's people were, by Satanic influence, tempted to slack their confidence in prayer." After returning from a Union prisoner-of-war camp to a prostrated Charleston, Girardeau responded at Zion Presbyterian Church on Glebe Street by offering a sermon on prayer from Luke 18:1 ("Men ought always to pray"). He called for humility and submission to the God's providence in the Confederate defeat and the emancipation of the slaves. Unbelief, Girardeau told his congregation in 1865, is the greatest of all sins, for Christ alone saves men. He ended grimly, "It is a fearful thing to fall into the hands of the living God."

Preaching to a packed house, Girardeau assured Southerners that God had promised them rest from their long travail: "The heavenly rest is but the complement of that which the believer now enjoys in Christ." Reflecting on the War, he warned that no finite sacrifices could save sinners—that the will of Jesus alone would prevail. Making no specific reference to slavery, he spoke of the quest for rest from the tortures of "a guilty and accusing conscience." The revolutionary changes that were sweeping the South were mere dust: "The mysteries of Providence will no longer tempt to skepticism, and the perfect temper of submissiveness to the divine will, which is the result of the believer's earthly discipline, will forever preclude the excursions of the imagination which might tend to excite discontent even with a heavenly sphere of activity and joy."

Southerners, forgetting that the suffering of Jesus had been in-
finitely greater than their own, had arrogantly prayed for the
wrong things. They had failed the test of war but dared not fail
the new and even greater test of their own faithfulness.

In March 1863, Thomas E. Peck, a prestigious Presbyterian
minister and professor at Union Theological Seminary in Virginia, had delivered a message that Girardeau now echoed.
Peck uttered some fateful words the full import of which may
have eluded him. He predicted that God would deliver victory
to the Confederacy only if the people proved worthy of His
trust: "We have absolute assurance that he will withhold 'no
good thing' from them that walk uprightly. When he denies
anything, then he denies it because it would not be good."
Girardeau, too, continued to believe that God had ordained
slavery, and on that matter he also said more than he might
fully have understood. Girardeau told his people, "It is pre-
sumption to pray for those [blessings] which are contrary to
the divine will. If the objects of prayer be unlawful, the prayer
itself is illegitimate." Girardeau clearly did not mean that
Southerners had erred in praying for the survival of slavery, for
he never repudiated his early belief in its sanctification. Rather,
like many others, he was referring to a pervasive sinfulness that
did not stem directly from slaveholding but did have implications for the behavior of those who had been trusted by God
to care for their slaves.[49]

Those who sorrowed at the defeat of the Confederacy reflected deeply on biblical history. During the War, the preachers were fond of invoking the fate of Babylon as they struggled
with the words of Hebrews 6:4-8, which warn that judgment
begins in the house of God itself. For God inflicted an even

deeper humiliation on apostate Jerusalem than he inflicted on the pagan cities of the plain. When the Confederacy fell, bereaved white Southerners experienced the destruction of their cherished "Christian" slave society. As they struggled to read aright the signs of the times, they could hardly escape the thought that, once again, a wrathful and inscrutable God had called upon the heathen to punish His disobedient chosen people.[50]

CHAPTER THREE

In Your Fathers' Stead

And the Lord's anger was kindled against Israel, and he made them wander in the wilderness forty years, until all the generation, that had done evil in the sight of the Lord, was consumed.

And, behold, ye are risen up in your fathers' stead, an increase of sinful men, to augment yet the fierce anger of the Lord toward Israel.

NUMBERS 32:13 – 14

When all is said and done, white Christian Southerners failed the test to which, as they acknowledged, God had put them. To understand that failure, the roots of which lay deep in the structure of Southern slave society, we must look backward and forward from 1865: backward to the Old South's debate over the permanence of a biblically sanctioned slavery in the social order; forward to the New South's intellectually feeble and arguably blasphemous attempt to provide religious sanction for white hegemony and segregation.

Exposition of the scriptural defense of slavery, decade by decade, revealed a conflicted attitude toward its perpetuity. Even those who most passionately defended slavery did not agree on whether it would or should last forever. Many of the most prominent molders of public opinion hailed "Christian slavery" as a solution to the evils of the modern age, and, accordingly, they often talked and acted as if they believed in the perpetuity of the slavery practiced in the South. The most influential ministers indicated grave doubts about this prospect, although even they spoke in a cautious manner that invited misunderstanding. The slaveholders, for their part, congratulated themselves on their wonderful work in Christianizing the slaves and elevating them from savagery to civilization. Leading divines such as Bishop Stephen Elliott and the Reverend T. C. Thornton, president of Centenary College in Mississippi, encouraged the slaveholders in this regard, stressing that

Christianity was preparing the slaves for a freedom their masters would willingly grant in time.[1]

The divines differed among themselves, and many faced internal questions as well, especially those ministers who sought to contain the issue on racial grounds. Although many found diverse reasons for believing in the perpetuity of the slavery that they declared God had ordained, many others thought it presumptuous to hold that God could not withdraw His sanction in accordance with His long-term plan or, indeed, at His pleasure. Did not the Bible speak of Ethiopia's stretching out her hand to God? Were not the efforts of the churches and Christian masters converting blacks into good Christians and thus preparing them for freedom? Scientific racists, who asserted the biological inferiority of blacks, scoffed at the suggestion that they could progress to freedom, but the Southern divines despised the scientific racists. From Frederick Dalcho in the eighteenth century to Richard Furman early in the nineteenth to Thornton Stringfellow in the 1850s, the proslavery clergy held out hopes for eventual emancipation, usually tying it to colonization. If anything, the theologically orthodox Southerners proved more open to change than the theologically liberal did. The Reverend John Adger, an orthodox Calvinist, reminding his people that a miracle-working Providence intervened in human affairs, considered the possibility that God would withdraw His sanction. In 1849, he declared, "We count it almost profane to hazard one speculation about such hidden things of God." In contrast, the theologically liberal James Warley Miles believed that God revealed His laws through a science that was demonstrating permanent racial stratification.[2]

In 1822 the Baptist Richard Furman, acknowledging that blacks might progress, declared that, if they did, Christians would rejoice, much as they would rejoice at "seeing the state of the poor, the ignorant and the oppressed of every description mitigated." But alas, in the wake of humanity's Fall into sin "a considerable part of the human race, whether they bear openly the character of slaves or are reputed free men, will continue in such circumstances, with mere shades of variation, while the world continues." The difficulty plagued the proslavery divines thereafter. Among the Presbyterians, in the 1850s the Reverend Frederick A. Ross of Huntsville, Alabama, not only defended slavery but declared it a sound labor system regardless of the race of the laborers. Yet he opened *Slavery Ordained of God* by chiding those who insisted that slavery would last forever: "Let the Southern Christian—nay the Southern man of every grade—comprehend that *God never intended the relation of master and slave to be perpetual.*" The Reverend George D. Armstrong of Norfolk, Virginia, insisted that, while Christians cannot condemn as sinful a social relation sanctioned in the Bible, they must recognize that God might choose to do away with slavery in time. The Reverend Benjamin Morgan Palmer of New Orleans, whose widely circulated sermon rallied the Mississippi Valley to the secessionists, assured inquirers that he had never intended to advocate the perpetuity of slavery but, rather, that he had insisted upon the immediate duty of Southerners to preserve and transmit it.[3]

Southern reformers had to tread cautiously, for they had long argued that the Abrahamic household created a moral ideal for the master-slave relation and that Christianity accepted slavery as part of the general law of property and state power. The reformers also argued that slavery, like serfdom afterward, disappeared in response to economic pressures, not in response to Christian teaching. According to Sir Moses Finley, among other modern historians, Christian influence, in practice, therefore strengthened slavery, which is what the Southern slaveholders had always said. The Stoic philosophers, notably Epictetus and Seneca, protested the cruelties of slavery but nonetheless counseled obedience to masters. Finley comments that neither the New Testament nor the church fathers improved much on the rhetoric of the Stoics. But even when the Southern divines grudgingly conceded that the Stoicism exercised a greater influence than Christianity—or at least a prior one—in reducing the injustice and dehumanization of slavery, they could claim credit, much as Paul Tillich would do in the twentieth century. "It was (and is)," Tillich wrote, "the Spiritual Presence which acted through the philosophers of Stoic provenience."[4]

Virtually all proslavery theorists, Northern as well as Southern, argued that Christianity promoted a more humane treatment of slaves, but these theorists questioned the religious influence on emancipation. Samuel Seabury spoke for most when he denied that Christianity had much to do with the emancipation of the slaves either in ancient Rome or in the northern states of the American Union. Emancipation, he wrote, followed the dictates of economics. Thomas Roderick Dew pointed out that while the medieval Church did encourage emancipation, it made little effort to emancipate its own numerous slaves. Thomas R. R. Cobb, noting that slavery remained legal until modern times, agreed that Christianity softened slavery in Europe but doubted the Church's role in emancipation. Indeed, Southerners, with an assist from some proslavery Northerners, repeatedly asserted that opportunities for greater profit propelled a rapacious bourgeoisie to destroy serfdom and that the progress of capitalism destroyed the praiseworthy traditional loyalty of the peasants to their lords.[5]

Southerners had neither arrived at a consensus on the perpetuity of slavery nor divided into two rigid camps. Shadings, doubts, and ambiguities marked both sides of the debate, which united in a commitment to the perpetuity of racial stratification. With only an occasional exception, all believed that racial differences, even if determined by history and culture rather than biology, prevented whites and blacks from functioning as political and social equals. That is, they did not believe that, in the foreseeable future, emancipated blacks would be competent to function as responsible citizens of a republic. Terminological confusion accounts for much of the ambiguity. The participants spoke of *slavery,* but they often meant different things. Only those who considered blacks biologically inferior—a small minority among those who framed the debate in the South—thought that slavery per se need be perpetual. The great majority of the divines and secular leaders considered the possibility that slavery, as then practiced in the South, would give way to a milder form of personal servitude and racial dictatorship.

The replacement of slavery by the free-labor system never became a serious issue. Not even many of the full-blown emancipationists thought that the free-labor system was desirable, much less that blacks could survive in the marketplace in competition with white wage laborers. Nor did they think that blacks and whites could live together as social and political equals. Hence, they advocated the removal of emancipated blacks to Africa or elsewhere. Since most participants in the debates rejected colonization schemes as impracticable, they toyed with alternate systems of labor organization and social control. We shall examine their ideas in chapter 4. For the moment, let it be noted that the divines, supported by leading jurists and others, implicitly and often explicitly, acknowledged that radical changes had to be made in the social system if the slaveholders were to meet God's challenge.

The readiness of divines, secular theorists, and even politicians to consider substantial changes in social relations should have positioned them to guide postwar developments, but it did not. Recall that they grounded their commitment to slavery in an orthodox reading of Scripture, which led them beyond the defense of slavery to an attack on the free-labor system and to an insistence upon some form of personal servitude as the necessary basis for a Christian society. After the War, the churches, in their struggle to survive and rebuild, had to submit to and even justify the free-labor system and the attendant capitalist culture they had previously blamed for all the evils the Confederacy had risen to oppose, including and especially theological backsliding by the churches themselves. For, as James Henley Thornwell and others had warned, theological orthodoxy could not flourish in a social system devoted to Mammon. The Baptist Churches seconded his concern, expressing fears that submission to the Yankees would generate submission to theological liberalism as well as to racial egalitarianism.[6]

Adherence to Christian orthodoxy did steadily waver after the War, at least to the extent that ostensibly orthodox preachers fell back on secular argumentation to support their political and social views. In part, the retreat doubtless flowed from political, economic, and social pressures to which the financially strapped churches were vulnerable because of their dependence upon Northern support. The consequences of defeat weakened the resolve of the clergy, and many of its leading lights, with or without misgivings, began to counsel acceptance of the North's capitalist worldview. The churches formally held to theological orthodoxy, but, increasingly, they tolerated dissident views of a kind they would have previously put down hard. This new spirit of compliance resulted in a subtle yet fateful shift in theology as well as ideology. H. Shelton Smith, in *In His Image . . . but,* and Charles Reagan Wilson, in *Baptized in Blood,* have argued for a continuity between antebellum and postbellum religious and social thought, but their assumption that Southern churches had always espoused the strand of racism dominant in the bourgeois North obscures significant changes in the place of race in Southern thought. Their valuable books project a straight line from the antebellum defense of slavery to the postbellum defense of racial dictatorship and segregation.

Before the War the divines had not rested their case on race. They had explicitly declared slavery scripturally sanctioned and ordained of God regardless of race. True, many divines did invoke the Noahic curse and the supposed black descent from Ham in an ideology that took deep root among the people, but Thornwell and Robert L. Dabney, among other prominent divines, regarded it with suspicion since neither the Bible nor science demonstrated that the blacks descended from Ham. And Thomas Roderick Dew and Edmund Ruffin, among prominent proslavery lay theorists, shared this skepticism.[7]

The Southern churches resisted the scientific racism that by

the 1830s was sweeping the North, fed in part by a growing
hysteria over miscegenation. Scientific racism had arisen during the Enlightenment, and, in the words of David Brion Davis, "It was the heterodox or the champions of anticlerical science who dismissed biblical authority and who suggested that
Negroes, having a separate origin, were a species separate from
man." By the 1850s much of the Northern Democratic Party's
press had gone over to polygenesis and scientific racism to
excuse proslavery or at least pro-Southern views. In 1858, Stephen Douglas declared in his debate with Lincoln in Ottawa,
Illinois, "I positively deny that [the black man] is my brother
or any kin to me whatever." But scientific racism clashed head-
on with religious orthodoxy, and the churches of the Old
South denounced it. The Southern divines held their people
to Christian principles on these and related matters, and they
lost their battle only after secularization combined with the exigencies of segregationist politics to create a radically different
moral atmosphere.[8]

Before the War the Presbyterian divines kept up a steady
drumbeat against the scientific racists, who touted polygenesis
and denied that blacks and whites constituted a single species.
Southern colleges, dominated as they were by orthodox Christians, refused to teach polygenesis, notwithstanding its considerable and steadily growing popularity in the scientific circles
of the North. Men sought eminence and distinction by linking
the Negro to the brute. Thornwell declared to a large throng
in Charleston in 1850, "But the instinctive impulses of our nature, combined with the plainest declarations of the Word of
God, lead us to recognize in [the black man's] form and linea-
ments, in his moral and religious and intellectual nature, the

same humanity in which we glory as the image of God. We are not ashamed to call him our *brother*." Thornwell praised the steadfast refusal of Southerners to embrace polygenesis and scientific racism in their struggle against abolitionism. A decade later he returned to the theme in Columbia, South Carolina: "No Christian man, therefore, can give any countenance to speculations which trace the negro to any other parent but Adam." He denounced the scientific racists as infidels. Indeed, they were no friends to slavery, for, like the abolitionists, they were flouting the Bible and stripping Christians of ground on which to defend slavery and all social order.[9]

Since, in practice, one could simultaneously reject polygenesis and still peddle virulent racism, it is tempting to conclude that the debate did not matter much. But it did matter. If nothing else, rejection of a scientific, in contradistinction to a cultural, theory of racial stratification undermined the idea of perpetual slavery. The Methodist Reverend H. N. McTyeire of Tennessee, a future bishop, provided a disturbing exposure of the real stakes in his *Duties of Christian Masters,* in which he portentously warned, "One of the natural and pernicious tendencies of arbitrary power is to beget a feeling in its possessor towards his subjects, such as could only *properly exist* if he and they belonged to different species. If we would discharge our duties to our servants, we must counteract this feeling." McTyeire's injunction to counteract the feeling that one's slaves belong to a different species cut to the very heart of the issue. For the human tendency to view slaves as there for the convenience of their masters exposed the limits of the slaveholders' resolve to behave like Christian stewards. Each time a slaveholder broke up a slave family, he inadvertently worked out the logic of polygenesis, whether or not he formally adhered to that doctrine.[10]

Theological orthodoxy emerged as the strongest bulwark against scientific racism. Led by John Bachman, Thomas Smyth, and James Henley Thornwell, the orthodox stood firm, but not so the theologically liberal James Warley Miles of Charleston, who supported slavery primarily as necessary to the proper ordering of race relations. Miles insisted that the Bible sanctioned slavery, but he admitted that it did not specify racial slavery. He deduced biblical sanction for specifically black slavery from the ostensibly scientific evidence that showed blacks to be an inferior race and therefore divinely destined to subordinate status. Miles ridiculed the abolitionist "assertion that the negro is 'a man and a brother'"—a swipe also aimed at Thornwell, whom he despised as an intransigent Calvinist. "No one," Miles wrote, "denies that the negro is a man; but the abolitionists never consider what *kind* of man he is." Miles knew the answer: a racially inferior man. Having granted a certain metaphysical unity among the several races, Miles protested against social policies predicated on their equal capacities.[11]

Miles understood that the South could justify itself to the North only by standing firmly on the doctrine of black subordination, which enjoyed as great a popularity in the North as in the South. Miles also understood that the biblical sanction for slavery, not being racially specific, justified the enslavement of whites. Since, to his satisfaction, ethnology and history proved black inferiority, he, like the antiracist abolitionists he was assaulting, appealed to the spirit, not the letter, of the Bible.

Miles's interpretation of history allowed him to see such historic defeats as the fall of the Confederacy as necessary preludes to greater things. He had no trouble in adjusting to a new era in which the white race would take up the burden of civilizing the colored races of the world. Miles's theological liberalism and emphasis on science led him to the higher criticism and on to an uneasy flirtation with the theory of polygenesis. Even before the War, he tried to reconcile polygenesis with the Bible. Insisting on the reconcilability of the two creation stories in Genesis, he asserted separate racial creations while he upheld the notion that God had endowed all races with a moral sense. Before long he was arguing that miscegenation might be considered the original sin that had led to a common depravity. The identification of miscegenation as sin, while occasionally heard in slavery days, became wildly popular after the War among those Southerners who believed that God had effected racial separation and commanded men to maintain it.[12]

In the postwar decades the South accepted segregation in its churches as well as in the rest of society, while the Protestant churches generally supported American imperialism's campaign to bring Christianity to the "benighted" colored folks of the world. It took little perspicacity to see that if white Americans had a solemn Christian duty to conquer, rule, and civilize the colored races abroad, they surely had the same responsibility at home—and vice versa. The churches accommodated segregation and assorted doctrines of inherent black inferiority, albeit with much internal strife and resistance, but in so doing, despite continued professions of orthodoxy, they ineluctably moved to secular ground.

Buckner H. Payne ("Ariel") and other worthies scored big hits with books that claimed scriptural as well as scientific grounds for the depiction of blacks as subhuman. Baptists generally condemned as heretical the denials of black descent from Adam, but they rushed to find alternate—and insubstantial— scriptural explanations for a presumed hierarchy of races. In 1911, Bishop Joseph Blount Cheshire of the Episcopal Church of North Carolina conceded that if the Confederacy had won the War, slavery would have continued indefinitely since the social and economic structure depended on it and since emancipation would have run afoul of the blacks' "intellectual, moral, and social conditions, qualities, and *natural capabilities.*" However inadvertently, Cheshire's projection moved the argument for the divine sanction of slavery from principle to rhetoric.[13]

While increasingly harsh racism flourished, the churches of the New South, despite no few heresy trials designed to check the spread of liberal theology, plunged into a long-ignored retreat from their loudly professed orthodoxy. Meanwhile, the preachers fretted over the decline in moral conduct, and the churches became more vigorous than ever in trying to clamp down on drinking, dancing, card-playing, swearing, frolicking, and the like. As Jack Maddex has suggested in recent papers and will demonstrate in his forthcoming book, the postwar Southern Presbyterian Church, which long prided itself on being the world's last bastion of Calvinist orthodoxy, was slowly drifting away from the orthodoxy it insistently professed. And the Presbyterians held out longer and more effectively than did the Methodists, Episcopalians, and many Baptists.[14]

Presbyterians like Thornwell, Dabney, and Palmer, as well

as Baptists like John Leadley Dagg and Thornton Stringfellow
and Methodists like George Foster Pierce and William A.
Smith, had long expressed alarm at the collapse of religious
orthodoxy in the North, especially the retreat from the doctrines of original sin and human depravity. While readily acknowledging the strong conservative current in the Northern
churches, they declared them overrun with "baptized infidels." Whether Calvinist or Arminian, the orthodox Southern
divines predicted that a Confederate defeat and Yankee ascendancy would usher in an era of theological liberalism and
a prostitution of the churches to a creeping infidelity. After
Appomattox, the Reverend Moses Drury Hoge, pastor of
Richmond's Second Presbyterian Church, wrote to his sister,
"God's dark providence enwraps me like a pall." Hoge had lost
hope for "a gospel guarded against contamination of New England infidelity."[15]

In ripping the North for its spreading liberal theologies and
thinly disguised Universalism and Unitarianism, the proslavery
Southern divines had linked religious heresy to political liberalism, egalitarianism, and social radicalism, with their out-
comes in family disintegration (divorce, promiscuity, prostitution) and unemployment, poverty, and social disorder. Above
all, Southerners insisted that theological orthodoxy and the hierarchical social structure to which orthodoxy corresponded
must be understood as something more than the defense of
traditional values within a liberal, free-labor context. From
these clergymen's perspective, antislavery could not be passed
off as a mere reform but must be recognized for the revolution
it in fact was.[16]

Southerners warmly congratulated Northern conservatives

for doing their best to hold the line for the old values but increasingly criticized them for antislavery views that subverted their own religious commitments. Even Charles Hodge, the leader of the orthodox Presbyterians at Princeton, whom the abolitionists unfairly characterized as a proslavery man, did not escape criticism in the South. For while Hodge and others like him denied that slavery was sinful (*malum in se*) and defended the Southerners' constitutional right to hold slaves, he, like most of the Northern conservative divines, decried slavery as a social system. Almost all of the religiously orthodox Northern conservatives supported free labor; indeed, Hodge voted Republican. Hence, they came under fire from Southern divines, who declared that personal servitude was conducive to a Christian social order. Theodore Clapp, the Unitarian pastor of New Orleans and an extreme theological liberal, joined Thornwell, Armstrong, Ross, Stringfellow, Smith, William G. Brownlow, and others in sounding like George Fitzhugh.

Southern divines, both Arminians and Calvinists, supported by leading secular theorists, grounded their defense of social stratification and political order in Scripture and theology, and they identified the free-labor system itself as the source of Northern spiritual and moral degradation. They attacked Northern conservatives not so much for theological backsliding—even Palmer did no more than warn of a dangerous theological tendency in Hodge's ecclesiastical doctrines—but for supporting a social system that undermined their professed faith. Conversely, the Southern divines saw a brilliant future for the South, and specifically for the Confederacy, because it boasted a social system that permitted Christian doctrine and behavior to flourish.

To be sure, the defense of slavery had long contained elements that could feed into the grand theory of racial imperialism that came to prevail in postwar America. The Methodist Reverend Samuel Davies Baldwin, who lectured to huge audiences in both the North and the South in the 1850s, envisioned a Caucasian alliance of America and a united Europe as the future masters of the colored peoples of the world. Dabney noted in 1858 that four-fifths of the world remained unconverted but that the wonders of modern science and technology were providing the churches with the means to carry the Gospel as far as China and India. The English language, he added, was becoming the instrument with which the Anglo-Saxons were doing God's great work of unification in Christ. Thornwell warmly praised the efforts of Britain and the United States to spread the Gospel to Asia and Africa. Even the antislavery Robert J. Breckinridge insisted that emancipation was necessary for the "unity of the race, and that of the white race in Kentucky." [17]

In 1860 the Reverend William O. Prentiss railed that William Seward and the Republicans knew perfectly well that slavery was necessary to civilization. They themselves, he argued, sought to spread a de facto slavery that subjected ostensibly free laborers to irresponsible capitalists: "Let them carry their hireling civilization to the Antarctic, if they will; let them colonize new continents, if they can; their destiny is different from ours." Prentiss envisioned Southern destiny in the colonization of the tropics, the civilizing of blacks, and the expansion of Christian slavery. Fifteen years after the War the Episcopalian Reverend William Nelson Pendleton of Lexington, Virginia, was still defending slavery on the grounds that God had sanctioned the dominion of superior races over inferior ones.[18]

At the beginning of the War, the Methodist Reverend John

T. Wightman, preaching at Yorkville, South Carolina, identified Americans as of the Germanic race, which had a mission to civilize the world. "Cotton is King!" he exulted, "the cotton trade keeps the Bible and the press under the control of Protestantism." Leaving no room for misunderstanding, he declared, "The triumphs of Christianity rest this very hour on slavery; and slavery depends on the triumphs of the South. . . . This war is the servant of slavery." [19]

E. J. Pringle, among many secular writers, read Tocqueville as arguing for the subjection of inferior to superior races as the natural condition of mankind and as justification for the civilizing mission of the white race. When he published his *Slavery in the Southern States* in 1853, Pringle had doubtless also read John C. Calhoun's similar judgment in the *Disquisition on Government.* George Sawyer questioned a literal reading of the Bible and fudged the separate-species argument. But he insisted that, among the world's races, only the blacks had failed to progress. John Fletcher, along with many other proslavery writers, assimilated serfdom to a broad pattern of virtual slavery and argued, in part following early-modern French theorists, that Europeans had progressed to freedom because of a racial superiority that now dictated their world domination. In 1851 the magazine of the University of Virginia's student Jefferson Society casually referred to Virginians as "the great Anglo-Saxon race, whose destiny seems to be to rule the world." Thomas R. R. Cobb, reading world history, concluded that when two races occupied the same territory, the superior would have to subjugate the inferior. And in 1858, R. E. C., foreshadowing the postbellum shift from proslavery to imperialism, ended a series of articles on "The Problem of

Free Society" in the *Southern Literary Messenger* by suggest-
ing that the ultimate solution of the social question would have
to rest with the racial dictatorship of the white race over the
colored peoples of the world. Along the way, Albert T. Bledsoe
attributed the social ills of Latin America to the mingling of
races, and James P. Holcombe thought British rule in India
"despotic but paternal & necessary."[20]

Even the intellectually rigorous Thornwell did not escape
ambiguity when he declared that the capitalist countries could
only solve the social question by adopting a version of
Southern slavery. He appears to have been ready to embrace
some form of personal servitude for white workers, but, whatever his intentions and the force of his logic, an alternative
reading remained possible and more politically probable: the
transformation of white workers into a free middle stratum between the ruling class and the subjugated colored peoples of
the world. There is no reason to believe that Thornwell envisioned what came to be called in a later era "people's imperialism," but others were already glimpsing the possibility. Especially in the late 1840s and the 1850s, filibusters like William
Walker and the Southern admirers of "Young America" had
moved well along toward a concept that merged proslavery
with the rudiments of a modern imperialism more readily associated with the transformation of capitalism after 1870. That
any such vision could be reconciled with the Bible must be
judged, to say the least, doubtful, and subsequent generations
of imperialists who tried scripturally to justify their course
plunged into rank bad faith.

Yet before the War, notwithstanding the allurements of a
fancied white-dominated world, Southerners did little more

than entertain themselves with dreamy speculations. Imperialism did not take center stage in proslavery ideology. Not until after the fall of the Confederacy did a racial-imperialist ideology emerge in full force, as the South adapted to the values and policies of a triumphant Yankeedom. Indeed, in essential respects, the Southern embrace of imperialism represented a substitute for—and a betrayal of—the ideals and visions of the proslavery worldview, although it was tailor-made for a New South bent on continuing the racial subordination of blacks.

Racial separation advanced steadily within the Southern churches after emancipation, and when blacks left, most whites, despite marked emotional wrenching, breathed a sigh at having been relieved of a burden. Blacks left in droves, in part doubtless to express their religious feelings in their own way and to develop their own institutions and leadership, but also because most whites who wanted integrated churches simply assumed that blacks would have to accept secondary status as wards of their paternalistic betters. That blacks departed was hardly surprising, especially since many openly expressed distrust of and hostility toward those who had sanctioned their enslavement. Yet whites, liberal and conservative alike, seemed puzzled by the harsh reaction of so many blacks to being assigned to an inferior position in white-dominated churches.

Racial separation accompanied a growing apathy among whites to the religious condition of the blacks. Notwithstanding fine words and presumably good intentions, Baptist missionary work among the freedmen lagged badly behind antebellum levels. More tellingly, it lagged well behind missionary efforts to the Indians and to some white immigrant groups. In Mississippi, for example, widespread discouragement led the

Baptists to forgo missionary work, and not until the mid-1870s did their efforts begin to recover. In Alabama in 1869, the Reverend William A. Stickney, long indefatigable in missionary work among blacks, confessed to being discouraged about their future. Blacks, he thought, remained overly emotional in their religion, grossly superstitious, and indifferent toward the Decalogue and Christian morals. Stickney's discouragement deepened steadily during the next twenty years. Jeremiah Jeter, one of Virginia's most revered Baptist leaders, declared that God had separated the races and instilled in each a repugnance for miscegenation. Jeter did not hesitate to express his horror at the prospect of "The *mongrelization* of our noble Anglo-Saxon race." With such attitudes rife among the more humane and enlightened representatives of the dominant white race, the capitulation of the churches to the principle of racial segregation throughout society hardly engenders surprise. But what generally goes unnoticed is that the capitulation to segregation flowed partly from a lapse from the theological orthodoxy that the churches were still claiming to uphold.[21]

In theology, orthodoxy provided a bulwark against liberalism's propensity to accommodate polygenesis and scientific racism. It is nonetheless true that many theological liberals bravely opposed racist policies, while many—perhaps a good majority—of the orthodox disgraced themselves. Here, the theological liberals may not have been reasoning badly, for their preferred doctrines did not necessarily require them to surrender to the reactionary propensity. Let us assume the validity of the charge that they were sliding into essentially secular argumentation. They, as readily as the racists, had a rich body of secular thought to draw on. In contrast, the theologically orthodox who fell back on scientific racism to justify their support for segregation were inadvertently—and with astonishing irony—abandoning their much-trumpeted adherence to the Word.

The churches' theological retreat had devastating political consequences. No postbellum defense of racial dictatorship and segregation compared in biblical scholarship and intellectual power to the defense of slavery. The proslavery divines may be criticized severely for theological error, but they cannot fairly be accused of bad faith, much less hypocrisy, in their scriptural defense of slavery. The same cannot be said for their successors' efforts to defend postbellum segregation. Consequently, we need to reexamine the relative autonomy and integrity of the churches of the Old and New South. For we may well find that the retreat of the postbellum Southern divines into theological liberalism was organically related to their retreat from a coherent social theory and worldview—that, notwithstanding the admirable efforts of many liberals to resist segregation and a renewed oppression of blacks, theological liberalism, as doctrine, bolstered political reaction.

After the War, orthodox Roman Catholics and Presbyterians for once could agree in charging that scientific racism was a ploy to discredit the Bible. The proslavery but antiracist Roman Catholic Bishop Augustin Verot denounced polygenesis before and after the War. Dabney assailed the "half-scholars in natural science" who implied that the Church had no warrant to carry the Bible to the blacks and who were flattering the whites into thinking that their own sins were minor. Yet even Dabney and other orthodox Calvinists wavered in the wake of Reconstruction. Dabney, who did not doubt the inferiority of blacks, never consciously embraced scientific racism, but his postwar invocation of lurid images of blacks' animal proclivities and sexual appetites reeks of a capitulation to that despised doctrine.[22]

Nothing is more disheartening than to see such firmly orthodox Christians as Dabney, who stood all his life on *sola scriptura* and turned to the Bible for guidance on every subject, plunge into arguments from sheer prejudice that hardly pretended to be scripturally grounded. Immediately after the War Dabney opposed ecclesiastical equality for blacks, and in 1876, he declared for strict racial segregation in education, noting that since blacks would soon be stripped of the right to vote, they would have little need for more than minimal schooling. More ominously, he added that if blacks were to be educated, racial amalgamation would follow. And Benjamin Morgan Palmer, who supported racial segregation in New Orleans during Reconstruction, slid into an ambiguity for which he had not been known in earlier days. To be sure, Christian resistance to scientific racism continued, but in 1911, E. H. Randle could ridicule "Christians who are leaving no stone unturned to find evidence of the unity of the human race." And it was the Southern Methodist Publishing House that brought out Randle's books.[23]

Decade by decade, church leaders frankly acknowledged that the sentiments of the white communities largely determined their responses to measures for segregation, disfranchisement, and the politics of race. The capitulation to a community sentiment that, in effect, defied Scripture proved one of the many joys of the steady—indeed, endless—democratization of the churches. Thus, in 1866 the Reverend Dr. Mc-

Tyeire, a future Methodist bishop, led a movement of younger preachers to curb the powers of the episcopate, relax discipline, and increase lay participation in church governance. The movement had begun in the 1850s, but it made little headway before the War, in part because of the strong opposition of the formidable Bishop George Foster Pierce.[24]

The churches did little to justify their segregationist course scripturally and theologically. Indeed, they did not have to do much more than accept racial separation within and between churches as a matter of course. Attempts to justify segregation scripturally and theologically fell back on the always frail interpretation of Noah's curse. Those who did speak up for segregation ended by invoking current scientific theories to support a theology that could not rest on the Bible without dubious extrapolations from ambiguous texts. When the great civil rights struggle opened in the second half of the twentieth century, the Southern divines, many of whom prided themselves on their Christian orthodoxy, opposed racial integration with arguments grounded in politics rather than Scripture. Martin Luther King, Jr., among others, severely criticized the Southern white churches for their failure to support integration, but, notwithstanding political pandering, the white churches provided the segregationists with little scriptural ammunition.[25]

Most ministers tried to stay off the firing line, but those who sought a religious basis for segregationist politics largely restricted themselves to a refutation of the assertion that the Bible specifically supported integration. Among those who argued the religious case for the White Citizens' Councils, Medford Evans and G. T. Gillespie did precious little with the Bible beyond refuting the weaker arguments on the other side.

Nor did the leading churchgoing politicians and journalists attempt to defend segregation on religious grounds. In 1957, the White Citizens' Council serialized and widely circulated a "Manual for Southerners." The first installment, aimed at third- and fourth-graders, said no more than that God created four races. It offered no biblical argument at all for segregation. The contrast with the impressive scholarly efforts of the ante-bellum divines to ground slavery in Scripture could hardly be more striking.[26]

The South African segregationists did no better, for all their vaunted reputation as theologically serious Calvinists. It would be preposterous to hold Calvin and Calvinism responsible for the emergence of racist ideology in South Africa or anywhere else, however much some Calvinists twisted the doctrine of double predestination to account for racial stratification. For the most part, the Afrikaans nationalists who promoted Apartheid extolled the community over the individual to an extent that resembled nothing as much as secular Nazi doctrine, although "scientific" theories of blood played little part in their thinking. The nationalists saw themselves as a new Israel, rescued from the bondage imposed by those modern Egyptians, the British imperialists, and forced to battle those modern Canaanites, the Zulus. Redemptive suffering became their main theme, for God chastens those he loves. The South African segregationists cited Genesis 1:28, Deuteronomy 32:8-9, and Acts, 2:5-11 and 17:26 to argue that God had designed the world to be filled with a diversity of races that were to live separately but in a hierarchical relation dominated by His chosen people—who, providentially, turned out to be white. Curiously, Afrikaans racists made little use of Noah's curse. In any case, their interpretations piled assertion on assertion in a manner that convinced only themselves.[27]

The persistent fear of racial equality explains much in the tortured history of the South before and after the War for Southern Independence, but it does not explain enough. That matters went from bad to worse after the War no one doubts. But why did the reformers of the Old South and the Confederacy accomplish so little while time remained? To that question we shall now turn.

CHAPTER FOUR

An Uncertain Trumpet

For if the trumpet give an uncertain sound, who shall prepare himself to the battle?

1 CORINTHIANS 14:8

When the Confederacy collapsed, the divines ruefully allowed that God had punished the South for failing to do justice to its slaves. Simultaneously, they reiterated their conviction that they had not sinned in upholding slavery per se. In October 1865, the Baptist *Religious Herald* of Richmond, Virginia, defiantly asked "whether any combination of capital and labor ever produced greater freedom from want and suffering, and a higher degree of contentment and cheerfulness among the laboring classes, than did Southern slavery." A month later, the South Carolina Conference of the Methodist Episcopal Church, in a pastoral letter, reiterated that Holy Scripture contains everything necessary for salvation and warned against a misreading of the fall of the Confederacy. It affirmed that the War had settled the question of "the powers that be," whom Southerners were commanded to obey as they rendered unto Caesar the things that are Caesar's. But the conference insisted that the demise of slavery did not invalidate the certainty that God had ordained it in a previous time and place. Educators like the Presbyterian Reverend T. E. Peck of Union Theological Seminary in Richmond firmly contended that, religiously and morally, slavery was by no means a settled issue. The intransigence of the divines may be more readily understood if for "slavery" we substitute "some form of personal servitude" and recall the long efforts to bring their preferred social system up to biblical standards.[1]

Christian Southerners, sadly acknowledging that they had lost the War because a persistent sinfulness had cost them God's favor, recognized a bitter irony. By forfeiting God's favor, they had sentenced themselves to live under the very social system that they had condemned as un-Christian in tendency. Punished for their lapses, they now found themselves enmeshed in a materialistic, marketplace society that promoted competitive individualism and worshiped Mammon. From early on, they had feared that defeat would ensure precisely that outcome. In December 1861 the Reverend J. Henry Smith of North Carolina declared, as others were doing in their own words, "If we fail, the progress of civilization will be thrown back a century." A still hopeful James Henley Thornwell pondered that fearful possibility in a letter written to his wife shortly before his death in 1862: "Every day increases my sense of the value of the principles for which we are contending. If we fail, the hopes of the human race are put back for more than a century." [2]

Thornwell could contemplate the possibility of defeat without loss of the optimism of the will that Romain Rolland has wisely suggested must accompany pessimism of the intellect, but not all of his compatriots could match his confidence in the ultimate triumph of the principles for which they were contending. When the prospects for a Union victory mounted after Gettysburg and Vicksburg, ministers and secular leaders continued to express confidence in a Confederate victory, but a note of desperation crept into their sermons. Haunted by fears of a religious as well as social and political catastrophe, the preachers redoubled their efforts to rally the faithful, but, notwithstanding the growing doubts, they continued to resist the idea of slavery's inherent sinfulness. Instead, they reiterated their belief that slavery, with all its faults, sustained a Christian social order, and they focused on the dreaded consequences of the victory of the Antichrist. Southerners must trust God to save them, the preachers cried, for the Yankee invaders have shown how utterly bestial they can be. The preachers reminded their people that an infidel North stood for a political radicalism that threatened the very foundations of civilization. If the North wins, they prophesied, the country will fall under a ruthless tyranny that will, among other atrocities, extinguish religious liberty and, with it, religious truth.[3]

At the end of the War, the unreconstructed Robert L. Dabney suffered such deep discouragement that he considered emigration. Virginia, he wrote to the Reverend Moses Drury Hoge in August 1865, will no doubt recover its prosperity but only at the price of "being completely Yankeeized." The loss of independence meant that "the honor, the hospitality, the integrity, everything which constituted Southern character is gone forever." The Yankees, he added, are killing off the "ruling class." In 1868, speaking at Davidson College in North Carolina, Dabney referred to the Confederate defeat as one more proof that God uses infidels to chasten His people, and Dabney reiterated that victory in war does not always go to the cause of right. Dabney, to the day he died, hated the bourgeois social order the slave South had stood against, but he wound up supporting big business against both Populism and the labor unions as the lesser of unspeakable evils. Dabney was not alone in being haunted by apocalyptic visions, which marked the sermons of many divines shortly after the War. For men like the less politically volatile Reverend John Girardeau, the emergence of socialism, anarchism, and class warfare in Europe and America conjured up the specter of the Antichrist. Without the religious overtones, the embittered Eliza Frances Andrews of Georgia cried, "In another generation or two, this beautiful country of ours will have lost its distinctive civilization and become no better than a nation of Yankee shopkeepers."[4]

The question remains: What went wrong? Why did the many Southerners who long before the War saw the need for a drastic change in the social order fail so miserably? After all, their ranks included politically influential clerical and secular spokesmen of high intellectual quality. That question leads to another: With all the good will in the world, could the slaveholders, as a class, ever have countenanced the kind of reforms that were being urged upon them by their pastors and their own Christian consciences?

Let us begin by recalling the paradoxical juxtaposition of common beliefs in the Southern attitude toward the perpetuation of slavery: first, slavery, as practiced in the South, might not last forever; second, slavery was an immeasurably better, more Christian system than free labor; and third, the Southern slave system cried out for radical reform. Thornwell provided a jarring illustration of the paradox. As forcefully as any Southern divine, he excoriated the free-labor system and regarded its expected demise as a moral, political, and social imperative. Yet according to Benjamin Morgan Palmer, Thornwell was drafting a plan for gradual emancipation in an eleventh-hour effort to head off disunion. Then, too, in 1864, Mary Chesnut heard Palmer deliver a sermon in which he thanked God that slavery was doomed. Now, how could Thornwell and Palmer, honest and clear-thinking men, have simultaneously praised slavery as a superior labor system, damned the free-labor system as morally monstrous and politically insupportable, and looked kindly on the prospects for emancipation?[5]

Some Southerners understood the biblical sanction of slavery as absolute and binding on all future generations until the millennium, but those who demurred did more than remind themselves that God could withdraw His sanction if He chose. They warned that He should be expected to do so if the Southern social system were not brought up to the highest biblical standards. For God had ordained slavery as a trust, not a sinecure, and those entrusted with it had to meet heavy responsibilities. The apparent contradiction disappears once we recognize that, for Southerners, emancipation did not imply freedom, as others understood it. Southerners were by no means predicting, much less advocating, an emancipation that would throw into the marketplace blacks, whom they regarded as racially inferior, or, for that matter, the laboring classes of the white race, whom they regarded as also in need of paternalistic protection. The divines foresaw a stratified order based on the strict subordination of the laboring classes and the legally enforced personal responsibility of a master class toward those who labored for them. In effect, they foresaw a transition to a different form of bound labor, whether called slavery or not.[6]

Many of the divines envisioned a paternalistic personal servitude in which white as well as black laborers could be assured of their "human rights" while they submitted to the control of individual superiors. But unlike Henry Hughes of Mississippi in his *Treatise on Sociology* (1854), no divine tried to envision a socioeconomic system that could encompass the recommended reforms. That some such system would have been acceptable either to Southerners or to Northerners may be doubted, and Thornwell's desperate hopes of avoiding secession and war may well have been sheer fantasy. Certainly, the problems were daunting. Thus, in 1858, James P. Holcombe cautiously suggested to the State Agricultural Society of Virginia that slavery could be maintained in a manner that held black families together, but he offered no specifics. Holcombe, like other educated Southerners, knew that the Spartan helots provided an illustration of communally owned slaves with family rights, but they also knew that a system of helotry was by no means a system of slavery as established in Athens, Rome, or the South. For that matter, they knew how brutally the Spartans treated their helots despite formal recognition of family rights.[7]

The vision of a reformed Southern social system had nonetheless long been building. Some Southerners could speak of "emancipation" because they were assuming a transition to a social order that had little resemblance to the "freedom" understood by the ideology prevalent in the North and in Great Britain. For some time, critics of slavery had been flirting with notions of a transformation in the social system short of straightforward abolition. In 1832, John Pendleton Kennedy, a Unionist Marylander, suggested in *Swallow Barn*, as Harriet Beecher Stowe would do in *Dred* some twenty years later, that Southern slavery could or should evolve into a kind of villeinage in which a peasantry would depend on the protection of paternalistic lords. In 1833, the antislavery John Greenleaf Whittier thought that slavery might well evolve into a system of serfdom of the Russian or Polish variety. Whittier insisted that freedom burned in the hearts of all men, rejected schemes to colonize blacks abroad, and denounced "ameliorization," observing, "It is impossible to perceive either its justice or expediency." William Goodell, an abolitionist, even suggested, probably tongue-in-cheek, that the slave states ought to declare slaves real property and restore entail and thus prevent the breakup of families by binding them to the soil.[8]

Support for some such reform came from Thomas Carlyle, whom Southerners immensely admired for his social and political views despite widespread distrust of his idiosyncratic religious views. In 1851, Nathaniel Beverley Tucker asked Carlyle to speak out in the support of the cause of the South. Carlyle's reply began well enough: He denounced abolitionism as "the keynote of that huge anarchic roar, now rising in all nations, for good reasons too—which tends to abolish all mastership and obedience, whatsoever in this world, and to render society impossible among the sons of Adam!" But Carlyle then suggested that a system of servitude for life would be preferable to the kind of slavery that existed in the South, and he pointedly asked whether Southern law permitted slaves to earn money to buy their freedom. While courteous and indirect, his remarks left no doubt that he thought the Southern system badly in need of reformation. From the point of view of the intransigent supporters of slavery, the great trouble with Carlyle's musings was that they pointed less toward a reformation of slavery than toward a metamorphosis into a radically different kind of social order. But many other Southerners who were no less loyal to the slaveholders' regime thought that such a transformation would not be a bad thing. In truth, it was what they had in mind all along.[9]

In one way or another, thoughtful Southerners writhed over

the gap between the realities of slavery and an ideal system of servitude they considered biblically sanctioned. The divines and jurists preached the model of the Abrahamic household and respect for the human rights of servile laborers, for they knew that the slaveholders' performance fell far short of their professed standards. And as Kennedy, Stowe, and Whittier perceived, the logic of the proslavery reformers' program pointed toward a system of bond labor rather than of free labor.

Toward the end of the War, Judah P. Benjamin, the Confederate secretary of state, undertook the difficult role of point man for Jefferson Davis in response to those who were calling for the recruitment of black troops in exchange for their emancipation. Benjamin's remarks plainly laid out the kind of regime that an increasing number of slaveholders were coming to see as the social system of the future. Southerners, Benjamin wrote to his friend Frederick Porcher of South Carolina, should seek "to modify and ameliorate the existing condition of that inferior race by providing it certain legal rights of property, a certain degree of personal liberty, and legal protection for the marital and parental relations, . . . to relieve our institutions from much that is not only unjust and impolitic in itself, but calculated to draw upon us the odium and reprobation of civilized man." [10]

Yet the invocation of "legal protection for the marital and parental relations" exposed, as much as anything, the difficulties the reformers faced. Two main types of proposals emerged: those designed to place slaves beyond seizure for debt, and those designed to bind the slaves to the land, regardless of the fortunes of specific owners. In 1836 the high court of Tennessee refused to permit the heirs of slave property to break a will that required them to keep the slaves at home. The heirs, invoking property rights, wanted to take the slaves to Mississippi, where their labor would be more profitable. The words of Judge William Reese had little lasting juridical impact, but they qualified as an ideological straw in the wind. He invoked "protective public sentiment to the slave," explaining that in Tennessee "the annual profit of the slave's labor bears no very large proportion to his value," and "the slave may not be overworked," whereas in Mississippi "the annual profit may be one third of his entire value, and the temptation would be to overwork him." [11]

Pressure mounted to exempt at least some slaves from seizure for debt. Although encouraged in the first instance by a wish to strengthen the slaveholding interest rather than by a concern for the slaves, acceptance of the principle would have shifted the concept of slave property in favor of the protection of the slaves. In 1853 the Alabama legislature considered a bill to exempt slaves from sale under execution, and the *Southern Cultivator* saw much merit in a proposal that would more firmly bind slaves to their masters. In 1857, Alabama Governor John A. Winston urged, "By the exemption of one slave, at least, from the process of the law, and his increase, if female, the investment of money in that kind of property will be preferred to all others." John Archibald Campbell, a proslavery justice of the U.S. Supreme Court who chose to return to Alabama in 1861, confronted the wider issue and reiterated his long-standing ideas. The liability of the slave to sale for the master's debt, he charged, constituted a threat to the Christian and patriarchal character of the social system. Campbell expressed particular concern for the integrity of the slave family and wanted prohibition of its disruption by sale. But his larger argument focused on unity of "the family, white and black," and he demanded that the law place every possible obstacle in the way of the separation of slaves from masters in financial difficulties.[12]

In Louisiana, Samuel Walker, a large sugar planter, fretting over the size of the Republican vote in the presidential election of 1856, sought to arouse his fellow slaveholders to strengthen their regime and repel antislavery attacks. He proposed to exempt slaves from seizure and sale for debt and thereby make the slave family secure and encourage slave ownership among the yeomen. His suggestion that slaves become the permanent and nonalienable property of the family that owned them attracted the interest if not the assent of J. D. B. DeBow, among others. Prominent members of the legal profession showed increasing interest in such proposals. Judge John Belton O'Neall of South Carolina protested the insecurity of the slaves in the face of the existing property laws and wanted them attached to freeholds.[13]

Upon reflection, DeBow joined Louisa McCord and others in attacking proposals for protecting slaves by binding them to the soil, arguing that any such system would actually lead to a deterioration in the condition of the blacks and to their destruction. In effect, DeBow and McCord were reminding their colleagues of the long-standing Southern argument that blacks could not take care of themselves and needed protection in the economic competition of the marketplace. McCord denounced Henry Carey's proposal to transform Southern slaves into *ad-scripti glebae,* for it "would tie the poor negro to the soil, there to suffer under the pinching rule of want, for both master and slave, until the master, driven away, starved out, leaves the negro to his freedom and his pursuing fate." To Carey's suggestion that economic progress would bring rising food prices, McCord raged that, in consequence, masters would abandon care of black children to their fathers: "Here is progress! The negro is too comfortable in his slavery; make him a freeman; let him suffer a *greater sacrifice* for the 'raising' of his children." [14]

The War brought the issue to a head. The Confederacy may have come into being as a bastion of constitutionalism, state rights, and traditional values, as its originators and many others since have claimed with considerable justification, but it also came into being as a slaveholding republic. Alexander H. Stephens could not have been clearer in his "Cornerstone Speech," and no Southerner of importance contradicted him. Yet, almost from the opening shot at Fort Sumter, the future of slavery in a victorious Confederacy became the subject of heated debate, for the calls to bring slavery up to biblical standards would have effected a social revolution. In 1863, an anonymous writer in *Southern Presbyterian Review,* replying to James Lyon and the Presbyterian reformers, warmly endorsed most of their proposals but demurred on slave marriages. Legalization of slave marriages would grant the right of contract to slaves and thereby destroy the master's patriarchal control: "It would amount to a revolution in the status of the slave as great as a transfer of allegiance from one prince or state to another would effect in the condition of a free people." That step, he insisted, would open the door to recognition of the slave's right to enter into contracts to accumulate property and much else. Some of this writer's arguments were tortured, but their principal thrust struck home: The essential reforms would undermine the master-slave relation in a social experiment that threatened the power of the master class.[15]

The reformers replied to their critics by insisting that a milder system of labor bondage would provide the protection that McCord feared would be lost. They were doubtless sincere, but they never did explore the ramifications of proposals that would have led toward a new social system. From antiquity, as educated Southerners well knew, slavery flourished only as a system of commodity production—production for market—whereas serfdom did not, at least not normally or necessarily. It is true that the emergence of large-scale serfdom in sixteenth-century Russia and the "second serfdom" in eastern Europe poured foodstuffs into the cities of a rapidly developing capitalist western Europe, but the deepening economic backwardness of the East offered little encouragement to those invited to plunge into the proposed reformation of slavery. For one thing, educated slaveholders were taught medieval history in school and read a good deal of it thereafter. And in the late Middle Ages, just as a vassal could turn to the king's court to protect him against a lord, so a serf could run to town not merely to escape his master's clutches but to secure legal protection against him. The belief in the supremacy and sanctity of the law rested on hierarchical assumptions that made both superior and inferior subject to mutual obligations and gave inferiors the right to appeal violations to an authority higher than the lord. The great difficulty in the way of a transition to a system of unfree labor other than slavery was that virtually all its features threatened the economic or political security of the slaveholders in a transatlantic world that was rising on commodity production for a burgeoning world market.[16]

Albert Barnes threw a favorite proslavery argument back in the Southerners' faces. Noting that the Southern divines insisted on defending the biblical sanction for slavery in general rather than the Southern slave laws in particular, Barnes argued, "It is not improper to regard slavery as it exists in the United States as a *fair illustration* of the tendency of the system. It exists here in the best age of the world, and in the land most distinguished for intelligence, and for wisdom in making and administering laws. The laws pertaining to the system here may be regarded as those which long experience has shown to be necessary." Barnes pressed his point: "It is hardly necessary to remark, what a modification it would make in slavery in this land, if it should become a settled principle that a slave could never be SOLD." The more moderately antislavery Reverend Rufus Clark of New Hampshire acknowledged the existence of many good and kind slaveholders but charged that the mass of slaveholders were doing nothing to mitigate the rigors of slavery. He concluded, "Were the Mosaic system to be applied to American slavery, it would be, by the operation of those laws, very soon abolished." [17]

Acute Southerners, opposed to as well as in favor of slavery, had long been mulling over the problem. In the winter of 1839-40 the Reverend George F. Simmons became pastor of a church in Mobile, Alabama, after having made clear his antislavery views. In May he delivered two sermons on slavery. The congregation listened with "attention and respect" to the first sermon on the Christian duty of masters to their slaves. But the second sermon on the evils of slavery and the need for a program of gradual emancipation led to his having to flee Mobile. He claimed that the trouble came not from his congregation or from the majority of the people of Mobile but from a "cabal" that had failed to have him indicted and then threatened to invoke lynch law not only against him but against anyone who defended his right to speak. Simmons believed that the majority of slaveholders, being inherently sinful like all men, should be expected to place their worldly interests first, so he aimed his appeal at the minority of the most pious, who could begin the work of reformation and spread its example. Simmons outlined the kind of reforms that would establish the Mosaic Law, which, while it tolerated slavery, contained no permission for the sale of slaves. Christians can only "own" slaves in the same sense that they may "own" their wives and children—that is, "they cannot be a part of our property; nor can they be treated as such." To reform slavery according to scriptural command, he concluded, would effect a fundamental transformation: "Thus will Christianity eat the heart of Slavery even while slavery continues." [18]

Simmons's challenge reappeared, if implicitly, in the efforts to reform the slave codes promoted by Judge John Belton O'Neall, who led judicial reformers in championing fairness for slaves and free blacks and in opposing obstacles to manumission. O'Neall's bold course led to charges that he surreptitiously held antislavery views—an error still echoed in the work of some historians who admire his courageous defense of the rights of black people. O'Neall made clear that he intended to strengthen slavery by providing slaves with security and the hopes for manumission as a reward for exceptional services. He called for kindness as indispensable, noting, "Nothing will more assuredly defeat our institution of slavery than harsh legislation rigorously enforced." Astute legislators and others saw the implications of O'Neall's bold program of reform and argued that it would lead to the collapse of slavery. [19]

O'Neall's critics were right. As both the more perspicacious abolitionists and proslavery diehards understood, the proposals to bring slavery up to biblical standards constituted, at least potentially, not so much a program for reform as a revolutionary program for the transformation of slavery into an alternate form of bond labor. White Southerners might have decided they could live with it since it did not necessarily threaten white supremacy and racial dictatorship, but some, notably the acute Louisa McCord, perceived clearly, while others perceived dimly, that any such transformation invited regional economic retrogression and the political decline of the dominant class. In the short run, the metamorphosis of the slaveholders into a new class of quasi-seigneurial landowners might not have undermined the power of those at the top, but it would have burdened them with a system ill suited to commodity production for a world market. It would have loosened their control of labor time, decreased the size of their marketable surplus, and, in general, undermined their ability to respond to market fluctuations. Later developments, coming in the wake of a crushing defeat in war, are no sure guide to the might-have-beens, but, along with the experience of postseigneurial Europe, they do suggest that no course of action could have prevented the emergence of precisely the bourgeois social order the slaveholders had long struggled to avoid.

A contradiction between intent and reality bedeviled Southerners who attempted to defend and yet transform slavery. Roman law established the concept of absolute property, which rationalized a commercial slave system based on commodity exchange. Roman law thereby provided an ideal starting point for the modern bourgeoisie as it fought loose from medieval notions of multiple claims to property. The Southern slaveholders necessarily had to claim the rights of absolute property for themselves, and they did so for the same reasons the Romans did. But Southerners simultaneously had to deny that they owned human beings outright and to claim only ownership of labor-power and services.[20]

Although George Fitzhugh and others proudly proclaimed their adherence to the idea of property in man, the proslavery divines and no few secular theorists adamantly denied that they held any such property. Their denial that they held property in persons hardly ranked among the strongest in the proslavery arsenal, and the abolitionists rent it simply by pointing out that, in practice, the degree of control of labor power the slaveholders claimed required power over the body of the worker. But the significance of this argument for the development of proslavery ideology, while virtually unnoticed by historians, should not be underestimated.[21]

Among other things, the claim that slaveholders held property only in labor and services exposed the extent to which the proposals to reform slavery implied a neomedieval theory of property. Historically, free and unfree labor have been associated with different forms of property, and, in modern societies based on absolute individual property, free labor has invariably triumphed. Modern slavery arose on the crest that brought absolute property to the uncontested status required by capitalist expansion. Benefiting simultaneously from property in their laborers and the freedom of commodities, Southern slaveholders did their utmost to garb slavery in older traditions according to which different people held rights in the same property.

The slaveholders tried to square the circle by claiming both the Roman concept of property and the medieval, notwithstanding their fundamental incompatibility. There can be only one Christian position on property and wealth, Dabney wrote: "Our property is purely a trust fund, and the whole of it is to be used for the benefit of the owner." The owner, he made clear, is God, and the human being serves only as the Lord's steward: "The owner, as a just and benevolent man, will of course allow his steward a competent subsistence out of the estate; but the profits of the property are his, not his servant's." Dabney added, pointedly, "The servant must be duly fed and clothed, in order that he may be able to work for his master" and avoid being "a dull, over-worked hack." Augustus Baldwin Longstreet took a more radical view and wanted to restructure the state legislatures to allow for the veto of legislation by representatives of such corporate groups as agriture, commerce, and manufacturing. Ultimately, the center would not hold, for the proposals to reform slavery exposed the harsh truth that the political and economic viability of the South or, more precisely of its dominant class, required the retention of property in man.[22]

The ablest defenders of slavery did not commit the theological error that would have God dictate a particular social, economic, or political system. They did not argue that slaveholders were exemplary Christians, whereas the employers of free labor could never be. Rather, slavery's defenders argued that slavery, milder forms of bound labor, or any other system based on organic social relations created conditions favorable to Christian behavior and to the spread of Christianity among all classes, whereas the demands of the market compelled people to choose between their Christian ethics and their material interests. Proslavery theorists thus merged "humanity" and "sentiment" with "interest." Recognizing the inherent sinfulness of man—his tendency toward selfishness and destructive behavior—they concluded that a social system must encourage the wayward to treat their dependents according to the Golden Rule by providing material incentives. That was the meaning of the constant boast that slavery merged capital and labor into a single interest. A slaveholder has a direct stake not only in keeping his slave alive but also in maintaining the good physical and moral condition that would enhance his productivity. The slaveholders read with respect socialists like Saint-Simon, Fourier, Owen, and Proudhon, although, to their cost, they did not know Marx, and, like the socialists, they assumed that in a society driven by the market, capitalists simply could not provide the stewardship of labor to which Christian capitalists might aspire. Northern conservatives, especially among the Whigs, believed that strong government could render capitalism much more responsible and humane, but they did not make headway before the War. Not surprisingly, the slaveholders considered them dreamers. Yet a number of the proslavery theorists became fascinated with Louis Napoleon's social program, interpreting it as a bold effort to subjugate and, simultaneously, to nourish the working class. In 1859, James Johnston Pettigrew, who knew western Europe firsthand, spoke well of Napoleon III as "really ambitious of advancing humanity," but Pettigrew warned that the "democratic element" that had helped raise Napoleon III to power "was calculated to cause as much apprehension as the enemy in front." Pettigrew concluded that Europe needed a "hand of iron." Southerners usually expressed disdain for this new despot who combined monarchy, demagogy, pseudodemocratism, bastardized socialism, and an iron fist, but they grudgingly acknowledged him as the man of order needed to contain the social question. Bishop Elliott, in accord with John Berrien Lindsley, hailed Napoleon III as a "great man" whose strongarm tactics kept "the discordant elements in the population in subjection." Others, while denouncing him as a tyrant, recognized him as the long-predicted military dictator who would restore social order to a deranged Europe, much as his great ancestor had done after the French Revolution. And besides, the proslavery theorists could hardly help chuckling when they saw a callous and arrogant bourgeoisie finally get what it deserved.[23]

The proslavery theorists did not have time to ponder the implications of a resurgent Bonapartism, and they fell from power before Bismarck instituted his social program in Germany. We shall never know how they would have evaluated the prospects for a welfare-oriented capitalism that enhanced the possibilities for a reformation under Christian guidance along the lines proposed in Pope Leo XIII's *Rerum Novarum*. We should not be too hard on proponents of Southern slavery for their failure of imagination. Notwithstanding the immense transformations of our own day, who is prepared to be sanguine about capitalism's ability to avoid the commodification of every feature of life and to promote a culture in which Christian principles can flourish?

As a matter of high probability, the new order envisioned by the reformers would not easily have been able to resist the penetration of Northern capital and, with it, the political colonization of the South. An independent Confederacy, bent on maintaining political and military power in an environment of nation-states embedded in a world market, could hardly have avoided the path of rapid industrialization and full-fledged capitalist development. Those who believe that a Southern Confederacy would have had to emancipate its slaves before long are probably right, but the kind of emancipation that Confederates were most likely to consider, in contradistinction to that which would have created a genuinely free labor system, promised to turn the South into a second-rate power. One way or the other, the slaveholders, however metamorphosed into a new class, faced a decline in their class power and an end to their dreams of an alternate road to modernity. At best, they faced the prospect of thriving economically as individuals who served as clients of Northern capital and who were subject to their cultural hegemony. We need not be surprised that they resisted the social restructuring toward which their Christian consciences beckoned them.

The failure of the slave system to reform itself—or rather, to transform itself into a more humane system of personal servitude—opened the floodgates to the absorption of the South into the mainstream of transatlantic capitalism. For the churches, that meant absorption into the mainstream of theological and ecclesiastical liberalism, although they waged a protracted, rhetorically fierce rear-guard action that long disguised the extent and depth of their retreat. The defenders of slavery had regarded orthodoxy as compatible with modern science and social theory but as a bastion against the anarchic doctrines of the radical Enlightenment and the French Revolution. That is, orthodoxy had been regarded as the foundation of a comprehensive philosophy and worldview that could master the modern world while resisting its theological and political heresies. And for the Southern divines, the prevalence of a comprehensive worldview required a Christian social system, which implied some form of servitude for the laboring classes. Let us thank God for slavery's demise. But however badly the proslavery social theorists, clerical and lay, erred in their proposed solution to the great social question of their— and our—day, they offered a profound analysis of the relation between the social order and the prospects for upholding sound Christian doctrine.

The Sixth Seal

And I beheld when he had opened the sixth seal, and, lo, there was a great earthquake; and the sun became black as sackcloth of hair, and the moon became as blood. . . . And the kings of the earth and the great men, and the rich men, and the chief captains, and the mighty men, and every bondman, and every free man, hid themselves in the dens and in the rocks of the mountains.

And said to the mountains and rocks, Fall on us, and hide us from the face of him that sitteth on the throne, and from the wrath of the Lamb.

REVELATION 6:12, 15–16

I have read the story of my own South," Thomas L. Stokes wrote in *The Savannah,* "of a beautiful and tragic story of men who built a way of life upon foundations of sand. For cruelty and jealousy, bravery and high idealism, all are mingled in the story of the Savannah."[1]

Nothing has loomed larger in that story than slavery. From colonial times, divines and laymen, Northerners and Southerners, whites and blacks, proslavery men and abolitionists all linked slavery to the will and wrath of God. George Whitefield and Samuel Davies, among many, accepted slavery but attributed the military and social problems of the colonial and revolutionary South to God's displeasure with the treatment of slaves. At the Federal Convention, George Mason of Virginia, describing every slaveholder as born a petty tyrant, cried that since nations cannot be punished in the next world, they may expect to be punished in this: "By an inevitable chain of causes & effects providence punishes national sins, by national calamities." More famously, Thomas Jefferson penned a scorching critique of slavery in his *Notes on the State of Virginia,* concluding that, knowing God to be just, he trembled for the fate of his country. Their voices did not prevail. Southerners, step by step, embraced the proslavery reading of Scripture and became ever more deeply committed to the way of life slavery made possible.[2]

The jeremiads, nonetheless, began early and never ceased, but none overmatched that which came in Darien, Georgia, in January 1739, shortly before the slave rising at Stono, South Carolina. Supporters of James Oglethorpe filed a petition against the proposed introduction of slavery into Georgia. They declared, "It is shocking to human nature, that any race of mankind and their Posterity, should be sentenced to perpetual slavery, nor in justice can we think otherwise of it, than that they are thrown amongst us to be our Scourge one day or other for our Sins: and as freedome to them must be as dear to us, what a scene of horrour must it bring about! and the longer it is un-executed, the bloody Scene must be the greater."[3]

A century and a quarter later, in 1863, the judgment prophesied in 1739 came to pass as the Union army arrived in Darien. The Yankee noose had been slowly tightening, and the majority of the town's five hundred whites had already fled ("refugeed"), taking most of Darien's 1,500 blacks with them. The citizens who remained faced a Union army led by General David Hunter but led locally by two abolitionist colonels who commanded black troops: the cruel, vengeful James Montgomery and the humane, idealistic Robert Gould Shaw. The Confederate army had withdrawn, and the citizens capitulated, asking only that their helpless town be spared in accordance with the accepted procedures of warfare between civilized peoples. Their plea went unheeded. Montgomery gave his blessings to an orgy of looting, which, however, was not enough satisfy him. Over the protests of an outraged Shaw, Montgomery ordered his black troops to burn the defenseless town. The troops did their work con amore. Doubtless, those black troops and the whites of Darien had never heard of the prophecy of 1739, whose instruments and victims they proved to be.

The prophets of Darien rejected the notions prevalent in their day and proclaimed slavery itself as inherently a sin that would bring down the wrath of God. The slaveholders, in contrast, considered slavery inherently sinless but deeply flawed by temptations to sin that had to be eradicated. At Appomattox Courthouse on a grim April day in 1865, the white Southerners who had confidently marched behind their Lord of Hosts encountered the consequences of their failure to meet the great test to which He had put them. On that day, many had to wonder whether they could ever have transformed slavery into the Christian institution they proclaimed it to be.

Pious, churchgoing, Bible-reading Christians had dreamed of a great Southern nation, and they fought for it with astonishing courage and tenacity during four horrible years of death and destruction. Mourning the wreckage, they were left to ponder the words of Revelation 6:17: "For the great day of his wrath is come; and who shall be able to stand?"

Notes

Chapter One. Waiting on the Lord

1. For the declaration of the Episcopal Church see Elizabeth Wright Weddell, *St. Paul's Church, Richmond, Virginia: Its Historic Years and Memorials*, 2 vols. (Richmond, Va., 1931), 1:141–47; R. N. Sledd, *A Sermon Delivered in the Market Street M. E. Church, Petersburg, Va., before the Confederate Cadets* (Petersburg, Va., 1861), 21; also Thomas Atkinson, *Christian Duty in the Present Time of Trouble* (Washington, N.C., 1861), 6–7; Alfred A. Watson, *Sermon upon the Festival of the Ascension, May 14, 1863* (Raleigh, N.C., 1863), 10. For a balanced account of the influence of the preachers in rallying public opinion to secession see Willard Eugene Wight, "Churches in the Confederacy" (Ph.D. diss., Emory University, 1957), ch. 1. Also W. Harrison Daniel, "Sermons," in *Encyclopedia of the Confederacy*, ed. Richard N. Current, 4 vols. (New York, 1993), 3:1398–1400. When Unionist preachers finally yielded to secession, they did so with gusto (see Mitchell Snay, *Gospel of Disunion: Religion and Separatism in the Antebellum South* [New York, 1993], esp. ch. 5).

2. Stephen Elliott, *How to Renew Our National Strength* (Richmond, Va., 1862), 5; J. S. Lamar, *A Discourse Delivered in the Christian Church on the Confederate Fast-Day, Friday, November 5th, 1861* (Augusta, Ga., 1861), 9. See also W. H. Vernor, *A Sermon Delivered before the Marshall Guards No. 1, on Sunday, May 5, 1861, at the Pres-*

byterian Church, Lewisburg, Tennessee (Lewisburg, Tenn., 1861), 11–
13; J. W. Tucker, *God's Providence in War* (Fayetteville, N.C., 1862),
6; George Armstrong, *The Good Hand of God upon Us* (Norfolk, Va.,
1861), 11.

3. For elaborations of the religious dimension of the proslavery
argument in relation to the "social question," see Eugene D. Genovese, *"Slavery Ordained of God": The Southern Slaveholders' View
of Biblical History and Modern Politics* (Gettysburg, Pa., 1985); Eugene D. Genovese, "Religious and Economic Thought in the Proslavery Argument," *Essays in Economic and Business History* 15
(1997): 1–10; Eugene D. Genovese, "Religion in the Collapse of the
American Union," in Randall Miller and Charles Reagan Wilson,
eds., *Religion and the American Civil War* (New York, 1998). Elizabeth Fox-Genovese and Eugene D. Genovese, "The Religious Ideals
of Southern Slave Society," *Georgia Historical Quarterly* 70 (Spring
1986): 1–16; Elizabeth Fox-Genovese and Eugene D. Genovese,
"The Divine Sanction of Social Order: Religious Foundations of
the Southern Slaveholders' World View," *Journal of the American
Academy of Religion* 55 (1987): 211–33; Elizabeth Fox-Genovese and
Eugene D. Genovese, "The Social Thought of the Antebellum
Southern Theologians," in *Looking South: Chapters in the Story of
an American Region,* ed. Winifred B. Moore, Jr., and Joseph F.
Tripp (New York: 1989), 31–40. On the Noahic curse see below,
ch. 3.

4. For Jewish views see Morris J. Raphall, "Bible View of Slavery, in *Fast Day Sermons; or, the Pulpit on the State of the Country*
(New York, 1861), 227–46. Raphall was a Northerner, but his sermon
was widely read and warmly received in the South. From a Southern
Jew see Samuel Yates Levy's poem, "Prayer for Peace," which speaks
of the South's manifold sins and God's chastisements (*American Jewish Archives* 10 [Oct. 1950]: 133–34). For Catholic views see "Domestic Slavery," in Sebastian G. Messmer, ed., *The Works of the
Right Reverend John England, First Bishop of Charleston,* 7 vols.

(Cleveland, 1908), 5:183–311; and Augustin Verot, *A Tract for the Times: Being the Substance of a Sermon, Preached in the Church of St. Augustine, Florida, on the Fourth Day of January, 1861* (New Orleans, 1861).

5. Augustine, *The City of God,* trans. Marcus Dods (New York, 1950), esp. books 1–4 and pp. 692–95; see *The Song of Roland,* trans. Dorothy L. Sayers (Harmondsworth, Eng., 1971); Edward Gibbon, *The History of the Decline and Fall of the Roman Empire,* ed. David Womersley, 3 vols. (London, 1994), 3:534. The uses to which Southern educators put ancient and medieval history and literature will be discussed at length in Elizabeth Fox-Genovese and Eugene D. Genovese, *The Mind of the Master Class* (forthcoming). But for an illustration from the pulpit: The Reverend A. M. Randolph told his congregation in 1861 that internal corruption, not the barbarians, destroyed the Roman Empire (Randolph, *Address on the Day of Fasting and Prayer Delivered in St. George's Church, Fredericksburg, Va.* [Fredericksburg, Va., 1861], 9).

Herbert Marshall McLuhan praised Allen Tate's poem, "Aneas at Washington," for drawing on classical themes to account for the defeat of the Confederacy: "It is no mere attempt to glamorize the defeated South by hinting that Negro slavery was like the rape of Helen, a wrong arranged by an army backed by superior force and calculating guile" (McLuhan, "The Southern Quality," in *A Southern Vanguard: The John Peales Bishop Memorial Volume,* ed. Allen Tate [New York, 1947], 106).

6. Bertram Wyatt-Brown, *Yankee Saints and Southern Sinners* (Baton Rouge, La., 1985), 165; Robert M. Calhoon, *Evangelicals and Conservatives in the Early South, 1740–1861* (Columbia, S.C., 1988), 59–60, 63–64; James D. Essig, *The Bonds of Wickedness: American Evangelicals against Slavery, 1770–1808* (Philadelphia, 1982), ch. 1; also Mary Stoughton Locke, *Anti-Slavery in America: From the Introduction of African Slaves to the Prohibition of the Slave Trade (1609–1808)* (Gloucester, Mass., 1965), 59–60; Larry E. Tise, *Proslavery:*

A History of the Defense of Slavery in America (Athens, Ga., 1988),
64; E. Merton Coulter, *Wormsloe: Two Centuries of a Georgia Family* (Athens, Ga., 1955), 32–34. As the divines well knew, the Bible
declared that abused slaves were entitled to freedom: see Exodus
21:26–27.

For Whitefield's course see Harry S. Stout, *The Divine Dramatist: George Whitefield and the Rise of Modern Evangelicalism* (Grand
Rapids, Mich., 1991), esp. ch. 6; George William Pilcher, *Samuel
Davies: Apostle of Dissent in Colonial Virginia* (Knoxville, Tenn.,
1971), 76, 110–13. George Berkeley, philosopher and later bishop, visited America in 1729, primarily staying in Providence, Rhode Island,
but also spending a short time in Virginia. He worked for their inclusion in the Church and for an improvement in their general condition, which he found disturbing (see Benjamin Rand, ed., *Berkeley's
American Sojourn* [Cambridge, Mass., 1932], 28).

7. Richard Furman, "Exposition of the Views of the Baptists
Relative to the Colored Population of the United States in a Communication to the Governor of South Carolina," appended to James A.
Rogers, *Richard Furman: Life and Legacy* (Macon, Ga., 1985),
quoted 283.

8. Richard Fuller and Francis Wayland, *Domestic Slavery Considered as a Scriptural Institution in a Correspondence between the
Rev. Richard Fuller of Beaufort, S.C., and the Reverend Francis Wayland of Providence, R.I.*, 5th ed. (New York, 1847), 128, 131, 135, 157.

9. Wayne Gridley, *Slavery in the South: A Review of Hammond's and Fuller's Letters and Chancellor Harper's Memoir on the
Subject* (Charleston, S.C., 1845; reprinted from *Southern Quarterly
Review*), 14.

10. Thornton Stringfellow, "Bible Argument," in *Cotton Is King
and Pro-Slavery Arguments,* ed. E. N. Elliott (1860; New York, 1969),
49; For a sample of slave testimony see Ophelia Settle Egypt, J. Masuoka, and Charles S. Johnson, eds., *Unwritten History of Slav-*

ery: Autobiographical Accounts of Negro Ex-Slaves (1945; Washington, D.C., 1968), 45.

The reformers had so many texts to choose from that they rarely cited chapter and verse. But see, for example, Judges 2:14: "And the anger of the Lord was hot against Israel, and he delivered them into the hands of spoilers that spoiled them, and he sold them into the hands of their enemies round about, so that they could any longer stand before their enemies."

11. For a sampling from the agricultural journals see James O. Breeden, ed., *Advice among Masters: The Ideal in Slave Management in the Old South* (Westport, Conn., 1980); also Chalmers S. Murray, *This Our Land: The Story of the Agricultural Society of South Carolina* (Charleston, S.C., 1949), 92; "Management of Slaves—Report of a Committee of the Barbour County Agricultural Society," *Southern Cultivator* 4 (Aug. 1846): 113. On Holmes and his friends see Drew Gilpin Faust, *A Sacred Circle: The Dilemma of the Intellectual in the Old South, 1840–1860* (Baltimore, 1977), 46, 100.

Hammond wrote to William Simms in 1850, "My religion teaches me that God often visits us with his wrath" (Hammond to Simms, Feb. 13, 1850, in *The Letters of William Gilmore Simms,* 6 vols., ed. Mary C. Simms Oliphant, Alfred Taylor Odell, and Duncan Eaves [Columbia, S.C., 1952–56], 3:15 n. 49). Frederick Porcher referred to slavery only implicitly when he cited the Bible to demonstrate that God punished the Israelites severely for disobeying his command to exterminate the Canaanites ("False Views of History," *Southern Quarterly Review* 11 [1852]: 26).

12. For a particularly strong appeal to the abolitionists to support the Southern reformers see Joseph C. Stiles, *Modern Reform Examined; or, the Union of North and South on the Subject of Slavery* (Philadelphia, 1857), 210–13, 239.

13. Alexander H. Stephens, *A Constitutional View of the Late War between the States,* 2 vols. (New York, 1970); see the documents in

Dwight L. Dumond, ed., *Letters of James Gillespie Birney,* 2 vols. (Gloucester, Mass., 1966), 1:210–22; Albert Sidney Thomas, *A Historical Account of the Protestant Episcopal Church in South Carolina, 1820–1957: Being a Continuation of Dalcho's Account, 1670–1820* (Columbia, S.C., 1957), 28.

14. R. L. Dabney to G. Woodson Payne, Jan. 22, 1840, in Thomas Cary Johnson, *Life and Letters of Robert Lewis Dabney* (Richmond, Va., 1903), 68, also 128–31.

15. Fuller and Wayland, *Domestic Slavery,* 160, 182; Charles Colcock Jones, *The Religious Instruction of the Negroes in the United States* (Savannah, Ga., 1842); David Macrae, *The Americans at Home* (1870; New York, 1952), 286–87. On the self-censorship of the preachers see James O. Farmer, *The Metaphysical Confederacy: James Henley Thornwell and the Synthesis of Southern Values* (Macon, Ga., 1986), 215, 220.

16. A. E. Keir Nash, "Negro Rights, Unionism, and the Greatness of the South Carolina Court of Appeals: The Extraordinary Chief Justice John Belton O'Neall," *South Carolina Law Review* 21 (1969): 141–90; George Tucker, *Progress of the United States in Population and Wealth in Fifty Years* (1855; New York, 1964), 43; "The Christian Doctrine of Slavery," in John Adger et al., eds., *The Collected Writings of James Henley Thornwell,* 4 vols. (Carlisle, Pa., 1986), 4:404.

17. John Taylor, *Arator: Being a Series of Agricultural Essays, Practical and Political* (1814; Indianapolis, 1977), 357.

18. On Ewing see B. W. McDonnold, *History of the Cumberland Presbyterian Church* (Nashville, Tenn., 1899), 410–16.

19. The South Carolina Methodist Conference quoted in Albert M. Shipp, *The History of Methodism in South Carolina* (Nashville, Tenn., 1883), 497–98; Ferdinand Jacobs, *The Committing of Our Cause to God* (Charleston, S.C., 1850), 22; William Meade, *Address on the Day of Fasting and Prayer, June 13, 1861* (Richmond, Va.,

1861), 9; also T. C. DeVeaux, *Fast-Day Sermon, Preached in Good Hope Church, Lowndes County, Alabama, on Thursday, June 13th, 1861* (Wytheville, Ala., 1861), 10.

20. R. H. Taylor, "Humanizing the Slave Code of North Carolina," *North Carolina Historical Review* 12 (1925): 330–31; William Harper, "Chancellor Harper on Slavery," in *The Pro-Slavery Argument as Maintained by the Most Distinguished Writers of the Southern States* (Philadelphia, 1853), 64–65. For some reports of cruel masters and demands for stern punishment see Lyle Saxon, Edward Dreyer, and Robert Tallant, eds., *Gumbo Ya-Ya: A Collection of Louisiana Folk Tales* (New York, 1945), 236–38; Ivan E. McDougle, *Slavery in Kentucky, 1792–1865* (Westport, Conn., 1970), 91–92; A. E. K. Nash, "Reason of Slavery," *Vanderbilt Law Review* 32 (1979): 39–40; Jean Martin Flynn, *The Militia in Antebellum South Carolina Society* (Spartanburg, S.C., 1991), 17; Ralph Betts Flanders, *Plantation Slavery in Georgia* (Chapel Hill, N.C., 1933), 241–43; Edwin Adams Davis, ed., *Plantation Life in the Florida Parishes of Louisiana, 1836–1846, as Reflected in the Diary of Bennett H. Barrow* (New York, 1943), 148, 202, 227, 239, 262 (diary entries for 1839–41); Frederika Bremer, *The Homes of the New World,* trans. Mary Howitt, 2 vols. (New York, 1853), 2:152; R. Q. Mallard, *Plantation Life before Emancipation* (Richmond, Va., 1892), 42–44; David Gavin Diary, Nov. 9, 1855, Southern Historical Collection, University of North Carolina, Chapel Hill. For the efforts of jurists, lawyers, and citizens to punish cruel masters at law see E. Merton Coulter, *Joseph Vallence Bevan: Georgia's First Historian* (Athens, Ga., 1964), 56–57; Francis DuBose Richardson, "Memoirs," 43, Southern Historical Collection, University of North Carolina, Chapel Hill; "Letter of Mary Woodrow to the Mayor of Alexandria, Va., June 21, 1813," "Slave Papers," Library of Congress; Mary A. Thrift to George N. Thrift, May 17, 1859, George N. Thrift Papers, Duke University, Durham, N.C.; "A Young Planter," "Communication," *Carolina Planter* 1 (1840): 209–10. For

some black testimony on white responses to cruelty see Egypt, Masu-oka, and Johnson, eds., *Unwritten History*, 2, 5, 103, 107; Jeff Hamilton, *My Master: The Inside Story of Sam Houston and His Times* (Austin, Tex., 1992), 23–24; F. N. Boney, Richard Hume, and Rafia Zafar, eds., *God Made Man, Man Made the Slave: The Autobiography of George Teamoh* (Macon, Ga., 1990), 59–161; Lou Smith in George P. Rawick, ed., *The American Slave: A Composite Autobiography,* ser. 1, 19 vols. (Westport, Conn., 1972), *South Carolina,* vol. 7, pt. 1, p. 302; Delicia Patterson in Julius Lester, ed., *To Be a Slave* (New York, 1968), 52.

In Mississippi, Governor George Poindexter enraged the religious community by pushing a harsh slave code through the legislature in 1822, and as a result he was defeated when he ran for Congress. See J. F. H. Claiborne, *Mississippi as a Province, Territory, and State* (Spartanburg, S.C., 1978), 384–88.

21. James Henley Thornwell to Nancy Thornwell, May 1, 1841, Thornwell Papers, University of South Carolina, Columbia; C. C. Jones to C. C. Jones, Jr., June 7, 1859, in Robert Manson Myers, ed., *The Children of Pride: A True Story of Georgia and the Civil War* (New Haven, Conn., 1972), 487–88; also Harold Wilson, "Basil Manly, Apologist for Slaveocracy," *Alabama Review* 15 (1962): 40–41. For extensive evidence of the efforts of ministers to reform slavery see Kenneth Moore Startup, *The Root of All Evil: The Protestant Clergy and the Economic Mind of the Old South* (Athens, Ga., 1997), esp. ch. 4; also Wight, "Churches in the Confederacy," 159.

22. Mary Burnham Putnam, *The Baptists and Slavery, 1840–1845* (Ann Arbor, Mich., 1913), 90–92; Wight, "Churches in the Confederacy," ch. 5 (quotation on 146). For the impressive Methodist missionary work among the slaves before 1845 see Donald G. Mathews, *Slavery and Methodism: A Chapter in American Morality, 1780–1845* (Princeton, N.J., 1965), ch. 3; also Donald G. Mathews, *Religion in the Old South* (Chicago, 1977), 136–37. For missionary work by Cath-

olics, Episcopalians, and Cumberland Presbyterians in the Southwest see James J. Pillar, *The Catholic Church in Mississippi, 1837–1865* (New Orleans, 1964), 34–42, 81, 85, 115–22, 268–75; Walter C. Whitaker, *History of the Protestant Episcopal Church in Alabama* (Birmingham, Ala., 1898), 80–83, 195–205; Elizabeth Silverthorne, *Plantation Life in Texas* (College Station, Tex., 1986), 158; McDonnold, *Cumberland Presbyterian Church,* 432.

23. Theodore D. Jervey, *Robert Y. Hayne and His Times* (New York, 1909), 370; Joseph Cummings, "True Dignity of Human Nature and the Evidences of Man's Progress towards It," *Southern Repertory and College Review* (Emory and Henry College) 1 (1851): 146–53; John Hersey, *An Appeal to Christians on the Subject of Slavery,* 2d ed. (Baltimore, 1833), 80; C. K. Whipple, *The Family Relation as Affected by Slavery* (New York, 1858), 12. Here and there someone offered the apology that, after all, Protestants considered marriage a civil contract, not a sacrament, but scriptural teaching could not so easily be finessed.

24. E. J. Pringle, *Slavery in the Southern States. By a Carolinian* (Cambridge, Eng., 1852), 32–35; Louisa S. McCord, "British Philanthropy," in *Political and Social Essays,* ed. Richard C. Lounsbury (Charlottesville, Va., 1995), 305; also, [A North Carolinian], *Slavery Considered on General Principles; or, A Grapple with Abstractionists* (New York, 1861), 18–19; *Southern Presbyterian Review* 16 (1863): 154–57; Julia Tyler, *A Letter to the Duchess of Sutherland and Ladies of England in Reply to Their "Christian Address" on the Subject of Slavery in the Southern States* (Richmond, Va., 1853); George Sawyer, *Southern Institutes* (1858; New York, 1967), 224. For a typical abolitionist reply see Charles Elliott, *Sinfulness of Slavery,* 2 vols. (1850; New York, 1968), 1:147.

25. George D. Armstrong, *The Christian Doctrine of Slavery* (1857; New York, 1967), 121–22; Robert L. Dabney, *Sacred Rhetoric: A Course of Lectures on Preaching* (Richmond, Va., 1870), 71. Al-

though Dabney's book was published in 1870, it contained lectures the substance of which he had been teaching for many years.

26. Verot, *Tract for the Times,* 12; Breckinridge quoted in Victor B. Howard, "Robert J. Breckinridge and the Slavery Controversy in Kentucky in 1849," *Filson Club Quarterly* 53 (1979): 336; Thomas R. R. Cobb, *An Inquiry into the Law of Negro Slavery in the United States, to Which Is Prefixed, an Historical Sketch of Slavery* (1858; New York, 1968); John S. Wise, *The End of an Era* (1858; Boston, 1900), 80–82. Jones reiterated his position throughout his writings.

27. John Brown, *Slave Life in Georgia: A Narrative of the Life, Sufferings, and Escape of a Fugitive Slave* (1855; Savannah, Ga., 1972), 55; Isaac Johnson, *Slavery Days in Old Kentucky, by a Former Slave* (1901; Canton, N.Y., 1994), 14; Macrae, *Americans at Home,* 213; Martin and Hall testimony in Benjamin Drew, *A North-Side View of Slavery: The Refugee; or, The Narrative of Fugitive Slaves in Canada* (1856; New York, 1968), 336–37. Black preachers in the North resorted to the Puritan jeremiad in their own cause, warning slaveholders to repent or face the wrath of God. On the black jeremiad see esp. Wilson Jeremiah Moses, *Black Messiahs and Uncle Toms: Social and Literary Manipulations of a Religious Myth* (University Park, Pa., 1982), and Theosophus H. Smith, *Conjuring Culture: Biblical Formations of Black America* (New York, 1994).

28. William Henry Milburn, *Ten Years of Preacher-Life: Chapters from an Autobiography* (New York, 1859), 350; Gibbon, *History,* 3:214.

29. On Memminger see Michael Johnson and James L. Roark, *Black Masters: A Free Family of Color in the Old South* (New York, 1984), 229–31; Messmer, ed., *Works of John England,* 3:257–58; on Flaget see Walter Brownlow Posey, *Frontier Mission: A History of Religion West of the Southern Appalachians to 1861* (Lexington, Ky., 1966), 194; Verot, *Tract for the Times,* 10; on Verot see also Michael V. Gannon, *Rebel Bishop: The Life and Era of Augustin Verot*

(Milwaukee, Wis., 1964), 40–41. On Elliott see especially V. S. Davis, "Stephen Elliott: A Southern Bishop in Peace and War," (Ph.D. diss., University of Georgia, 1964), 197; and Erskine Clarke, *Wrestlin' Jacob: A Portrait of Religion in the Old South* (Atlanta, 1979), 48–49, 69–78, 156–57. For the growing movement to protect slave families at law see Thomas D. Morris, *Southern Slavery and the Law, 1619–1860* (Chapel Hill, N.C., 1996), 437–39.

30. See "Table Talk," Dec. 10, 1861, May 8, 1862, in John Berrien Lindsley Papers, Tennessee State Library and Archives, Nashville. On the strengths and weaknesses of the reform efforts see Wight, "Churches in the Confederacy," ch. 5; David B. Chesebrough, ed., *"God Ordained This War": Sermons on the Sectional Crisis, 1830–1865* (Columbia, S.C., 1991), 239.

31. George William Pilcher, "Samuel Davies and the Instruction of the Negroes in Virginia," *Virginia Magazine of History and Biography* 74 (July 1966): esp. 293–94, 299; Wesley M. Gewehr, *The Great Awakening in Virginia* (Gloucester, Mass., 1965), 169, 235–36; *Shall We Give Bibles to Three Million American Slaves?* (n.p., n.d.), 2–3; Virginia Randolph Cary, excerpted from her book, *Letters on Female Character* (1828), in Joan E. Cashin, ed., *Our Common Affairs: Texts from Women in the Old South* (Baltimore, 1996), 176; Albert Taylor Bledsoe, *An Essay on Liberty and Slavery* (Philadelphia, 1856), 125–26. Bledsoe, an impressive theologian, had been an Episcopal minister before he wrote this book; after the war he became a Methodist minister.

32. Morris, *Southern Slavery and the Law*, 347–48; Marion B. Lucas, *A History of Blacks in Kentucky*, 2 vols. (n.p., 1992), 1:140–42; "An Old Citizen" quoted in George C. Rogers, Jr., *The History of Georgetown County, South Carolina* (Columbia, S.C., 1970), 183–84; on Texas see Randolph B. Campbell, *An Empire for Slavery: The Peculiar Institution in Texas, 1821–1865* (Baton Rouge, La., 1989), 175. On Georgia see "Act for Ordering and Governing Slaves" (1770)

in Mills Lane, ed., *Neither More nor Less than Men: Slavery in Georgia* (Savannah, Ga., 1993), 8; George G. Smith, *The Story of Georgia and the Georgia People,* 2 vols. in 1 (Macon, Ga., 1900), 354.

33. Charles Colcock Jones, *Religious Instruction,* 164, 183; Calhoon, *Evangelicals and Conservatism,* 152-54; Robert E. Corlew, "Some Aspects of Slavery in Dickson County," *Tennessee Historical Quarterly* 10 (1951): 224-48, 344-65; Joe Gray Taylor, *Negro Slavery in Louisiana* (Baton Rouge, La., 1963), 151.

34. Harriet Martineau, *Society in America,* 2 vols. (New York, 1837), 2:152; Harriott Horry Ravenel, *Eliza Pinckney* (New York, 1896), 24; Morton H. Smith, *Studies in Southern Presbyterian Theology* (Philipsburg, N.J., 1987), 51 (Davies); O'Neall taught Mary Veals to read, and she became a schoolteacher after the War (Rawick, ed., *American Slave: South Carolina,* pt. 4, p. 168); Moses Stuart, *Conscience and the Constitution* (Boston, 1850), 94; Roger Baudier, *The Catholic Church in Louisiana* (New Orleans, 1939), 238; Harrison Anthony Trexler, *Slavery in Missouri, 1804-1865* (Baltimore, 1914), 84.

35. Charles Lyell, *A Second Visit to the United States of North America,* 2 vols. (St. Claire, Minn., [1850]), 1:208, 267, 271; O. J. M. McCann to H. C. Nixon, Dec. 5, 1912, in Nixon Collection, Yale University, New Haven, Conn. Also Susan Nye Hutchinson Journal, July 1, 1838, Southern Historical Collection, University of North Carolina, Chapel Hill; Lucy Muse (Walton) Fletcher, Sabbath Notebook for 1841 in "Autobiography," Louisiana State University, Baton Rouge; Charles H. Moffat, "Charles Tait, Planter, Politician, and Scientist of the Old South," *Journal of Southern History* 14 (1948): 229; James C. Bonner, ed., "Plantation Experiences of a New York Woman," *North Carolina Historical Review* 33 (July 1956): 395; Katherine Chatham, "Plantation Slavery in Middle Florida," (master's thesis, University of North Carolina, Chapel Hill, 1938), 63-65; William L. Richter, "Slavery in Baton Rouge," *Louisiana History*

10 (Spring 1969): 125–45; V. S. Davis, "Stephen Elliott," 128. For black testimony on white efforts to teach them to read see Eugene D. Genovese, *Roll, Jordan, Roll: The World the Slaves Made* (New York, 1974), 563–64.

36. E. Merton Coulter, "Slavery and Freedom in Athens, Georgia, 1860–1866," *Georgia Historical Quarterly* 49 (Sept. 1965): 26 ("Old Citizen"); Charles L. Coon, ed., *The Beginnings of Public Education in North Carolina*, 2 vols. (Raleigh, N.C., 1908), 1:477–85, 502–3.

37. Genovese, *Roll, Jordan, Roll*, 561–66; Elizabeth Hyde Botume, *First Days amongst the Contrabands* (Boston, 1893), 4; "'Tattler' on the Management of Negroes," *Southern Cultivator* 9 (1851): 86–87; N. G. North, "Moral Culture of the Slaves," *South-Western Farmer* 1 (1843): 169. Jack Maddex, in his forthcoming study of the Presbyterian Church, will demonstrate that some leading ministers took a positive view of the learning capacity of blacks.

38. Harper, "Chancellor Harper on Slavery," 35; W. S. Grayson, "Dual Form of Labor," *DeBow's Review* 28 (Jan. 1860): 53; Willie Grier, "North Carolina Baptists and the Negro, 1727–1877," (master's thesis, University of North Carolina, Chapel Hill, 1944); H. Shelton Smith, *In His Image . . . but: Racism in Southern Religion* (Durham, N.C., 1972), 139; Ingle, *Southern Sidelights* (New York, 1896), 272; Stringfellow, "Examination of Elder Galusha's Reply to Dr. Richard Fuller of South Carolina," in *Cotton Is King,* ed. E. N. Elliott, 495. For the charge of wanting slavery in perpetuity see, e.g., Committee of the Synod of the Presbyterian Church of Kentucky, *An Address to the Presbyterians of Kentucky, Proposing a Plan for the Instruction and Emancipation of Their Slaves* (Newburyport, Ky., 1836), 9–11; Frederick Law Olmsted, "The South," in Charles Capen McLaughlin and Charles E. Beveridge, eds., *The Papers of Frederick Law Olmsted. Vol. 2: Slavery in the South, 1852–1857* (Baltimore, 1981), 252.

39. *Speeches, Congressional and Political, and Other Writings of*

Ex-Governor Aaron V. Brown of Tennessee (Nashville, Tenn., 1854), 14–15; State v. Daniel Worth, in Helen Tunnicliff Catterall, ed., *Judicial Cases Concerning American Slavery and the Negro,* 5 vols. (Washington, D.C., 1929–37), vol. 2, pt. 1, p. 33. On the Walker pamphlet and its reverberations see Peter P. Hinks, *To Awaken My Afflicted Brethren: David Walker and the Problem of Antebellum Slave Resistance* (University Park, Pa., 1997).

40. "A Mississippian," "Slavery—The Bible and 'Three Thousand Parsons,'" *DeBow's Review* 26 (Jan. 1859): 47; J. H. Hammond, "Letters on Slavery, in *Pro-Slavery Argument,* 124; Nathan Bass, "Essay on the Treatment and Management of Slaves," in *Southern Central Agricultural Society Transactions, 1846–1851* (Savannah, Ga., 1851), 196; "Management of Negroes upon Southern Estates: Description of a Mississippi Plantation Owner," *DeBow's Review* 29 (June 1851): 625.

41. John Adger, "Human Rights and Slavery," *Southern Presbyterian Review* 2 (Mar. 1849): 569–87; Jones quoted in George A. Rogers and R. Frank Saunders, Jr., *Swamp Water and Wire Grass: Historical Sketches of Coastal Georgia* (Macon, Ga., 1984), 52; on O'Neall see Nash, "Negro Rights," 184–85; also N. M. C[rawford], "A Southern View of Slavery," *Parlor Visitor* 7 (1857): 414–16; Rufus B. Spain, *At Ease in Zion: Social History of Southern Baptists, 1865–1900* (Nashville, Tenn., 1967), 85–86. After the War, Baptist leaders like the Reverend John Broadus of Virginia, in supporting at least the rudimentary education of blacks, reiterated their criticism of the antebellum prescriptions.

42. Ray Holder, ed., "On Slavery: Selected Letters of Parson Winans, 1820–1844," *Journal of Mississippi History* 46 (1984): 350; Jervey, *Robert Y. Hayne,* 371; John Belton O'Neall, "Slave Laws of the South," in *Industrial Resources, Statistics, Etc. of the Southern and Western States,* ed. J. D. B. DeBow, 3d ed., 3 vols. (1854; New York, 1966), 269–92. Also Cobb, *Inquiry,* 232–33; Clement Eaton, *Jefferson Davis* (New York, 1977), 45, 68–69; also Catterall, ed., *Ju-*

dicial Cases, 2:1–2, and the account of *State v. Levy and Dreyfous* (1850), 3:60; Charles S. Sydnor, "The Southerner and the Laws," *Journal of Southern History* 6 (1940): 11; H. Mattison, *The Impending Crisis of 1860* (New York, 1858), 34.

43. H. N. McTyeire, *Duties of Christian Masters,* ed. Thomas O. Summers (Nashville, Tenn., 1859), 100–101 (on marriage); 110–15 (children); 156–62, 185–92 (literacy).

44. Barnwell quoted in Steven A. Channing, *Crisis of Fear: Secession in South Carolina* (New York, 1970), 62; Anderson and Porcher quoted in Farmer, *Metaphysical Confederacy,* 11 n. 7, 239. For a sampling of the moderates' early pleas for peace see Henry Niles Pierce, *Sermons* (Mobile, Ala., 1861); Thomas Atkinson, *Christian Duty;* O. S. Barton, *A Sermon Preached in St. James' Church, Warrenton, Va., on Fast Day, June 13, 1861* (Richmond, Va., 1861); Emma Holmes's report on the sermon of the Reverend William B. W. Howe, June 15, 1861, in John F. Marszalek, ed., *The Diary of Miss Emmy Holmes* (Baton Rouge, La., 1979), 57.

Chapter Two. Give an Account of Thy Stewardship

1. For Harrison see Herman A. Norton, *Religion in Tennessee, 1777–1945* (Knoxville, Tenn., 1981), 63, 68; Rebecca Hunt Moulder, *May the Sod Rest Lightly: Thomas O'Connor* (Tucson, Ariz., 1977), 35. Not surprisingly, when Union troops caught up with Harrison, they sent him to prison. In 1861, Mary Chesnut sarcastically chided Southerners for thinking they were God's chosen people, for whom he was fighting (Mary Chesnut Diary, Nov. 11, 1861, in C. Vann Woodward, ed., *Mary Chesnut's Civil War* [New Haven, Conn., 1981], 233).

2. J. W. Miles to Mrs. Thomas John Young, [1861], quoted in Ralph Luker, "God, Man, and the World of James Warley Miles, Charleston's Transcendentalist," *Historical Magazine of the Protes-*

tant Episcopal Church 39 (1970): 134; John O. Beatty, *John Esten Cooke, Virginian* (New York, 1922), 89.

3. Drury Lacy, *Address Delivered at the General Military Hospital, Winston, N.C.* (Fayetteville, N.C., 1863), 4; Thomas S. Dunaway, *A Sermon Delivered by Elder Thomas S. Dunaway, of Lancaster County, Virginia, before Coan Baptist Church* (Richmond, Va., 1864), 7.

4. Dana quoted in Wight, "Churches in the Confederacy," 19; C. S. Fedder, *"Offer unto God Thanksgiving"* (Charleston, S.C., 1861), 14; on Wilson see Henry Alexander White, *Southern Presbyterian Leaders* (New York, 1911), 405. For a sampling of sermons with these distinct yet overlapping themes see Edward Reed, *A People Saved by the Lord* (Charleston, S.C., 1861); Joseph Mayo Atkinson, *God, the Giver of Victory and Peace* (Raleigh, N.C., 1862); David Seth Doggett, *A Nation's Ebenezer* (Richmond, Va., 1862); David Seth Doggett, *A Discourse Delivered in the Broad St. Methodist Church* (Richmond, Va., 1862); John T. Wightman, *The Glory of God, the Defence of the South* (Charleston, S.C., 1861); T. S. Winn, *God, the Arbiter of Battles* (Tuscaloosa, Ala., 1861).

5. Thomas Atkinson, *Christian Duty*, 7; William C. Butler, *Sermon: Preached in St. John's Church, Richmond* (Richmond, Va., 1861), 7, 10–12, 16–17; Lamar, *Discourse*, 8; S. H. Higgins, *The Mountain Moved; or, David upon the Cause and Curse of Public Calamity* (Milledgeville, Ga., 1863).

6. "Sermon on National Sins," in Adger et al., eds., *Collected Writings*, 4:510. Alexander Sinclair reads as if he were quoting Thornwell without attribution on the Temple of the Lord (Sinclair, *Thanksgiving Sermon, Preached at the Presbyterian Church at Six Mile Creek, Lancaster District, S.C.* [Salisbury, N.C., 1862], 12).

7. J. J. D. Renfroe, *"The Battle Is God's"* (Richmond, Va., 1863), 3–4.

8. Meade, *Address*, 6; John Leadley Dagg, *Manual of Theology:*

A Treatise on Christian Doctrine and a Treatise on Church Order,
2 vols. in 1 (1857, 1858; New York, 1980), 285; Dunaway, *Sermon,* 17;
Richard H. Wilmer, *Future Good — The Explanation of Present Reverses* (Charlotte, N.C., 1864), 6-7; Thomas Atkinson, *On the Causes
of Our National Troubles* (Wilmington, N.C., 1861), 5; Thomas Atkinson, *Christian Duty,* 12; Sylvanus Landrum, *The Battle Is God's*
(Savannah, Ga., 1863), 9-10; "The Apocalyptic Horses and Their
Riders," in D. S. Doggett, *Sermons, with a Biographical Sketch of the
Author by the Rev. John E. Edwards,* ed. Thomas O. Summers,
2 vols. (Nashville, Tenn., 1882), 1:49-50; Lacy, *Address,* 5.

Even when the Reverend John Paris breathed fire in a blistering
sermon on the treachery of twenty-two Confederate soldiers hanged
for desertion in 1864, he stopped to acknowledge, "War is the scourge
of nations. God is no doubt chastising us for our own good" (Paris,
*A Sermon Preached before Brig. Gen. Hoke's Brigade . . . upon the
Death of Twenty-Two Men* [Greensboro, N.C., 1864], 12).

9. Henry N. Tucker, *God in the War* (Milledgeville, Ga., 1861),
12-13; Sledd, *Sermon,* 17; C. C. Pinckney, *Nebuchadnezzar's Fault
and Fall* (Charleston, S.C., 1861), 7-12; H. A. Tupper, *A Thanksgiv-
ing Discourse Delivered at Washington, Ga., Sept. 18, 1862* (Macon,
Ga., 1862), 10; Stephen Elliott, *Sermon Preached in Christ Church,
Savannah* (Savannah, Ga., 1862), 11-12; Stephen Elliott, *Samson's
Riddle* (Macon, Ga., 1863), 21-23; DeVeaux, *Fast-Day Sermon, 3;*
Charles Minnigerode, *"He that Believeth Shall Not Make Haste": A
Sermon Preached on the First of January, 1865, in St. Paul's Church,
Richmond* (Richmond, Va., 1865), 7.

God is punishing Southerners, the Reverend T. S. Dunaway thundered in 1864, for being too proud, arrogant, self-reliant in their
boasts (Dunaway, *Sermon,* 8).

10. Stephen Elliott, *Samson's Riddle,* 14-15; Stephen Elliott, *How
to Renew Our National Strength,* 7; Alexander Gregg, *The Duties
Growing out of It and the Benefits to Be Expected from Our Present*

War (Austin, Tex., 1861), 5-7; T. V. Moore, *God Our Refuge and Strength in the War: A Discourse before the Congregations of the First and Second Presbyterian Churches . . . Nov. 15, 1861* (Richmond, Va., 1861), 6-7, 12-13. For differing interpretations of Elliott's views on war see Dwyn Mounger, "History as Interpreted by Stephen Elliott," *Historical Magazine of the Protestant Episcopal Church* 44 (1975): 286-89; and William A. Clebsch, "Stephen Elliott's View of the Civil War," *Historical Magazine of the Protestant Episcopal Church* 31 (1962): 19-20.

11. Robert L. Dabney, "The Christian's Best Motive for Patriotism," in *Discussions: Evangelical and Theological,* 3 vols. (Carlisle, Pa., 1967), 2:406-7; Charles Royster, *The Destructive War: William Tecumseh Sherman, Stonewall Jackson, and the Americans* (New York, 1991), 169-70, 268, 316, 415. See also the remarks of the Episcopalian bishop of Alabama (Wilmer, *Future Good,* 6-7).

12. Sermon, Nov. 23, 1862, in Otey Papers, box 2, Southern Historical Collection, University of North Carolina, Chapel Hill; Stephen Elliott, "Ezra's Dilemma," in *"God Ordained This War,"* ed. Chesebrough, 246-63; on Elliott see also Stephen B. Barnwell, *The Story of an American Family* (Marquette, Mich., 1969), 189; Gregg, *Duties,* 6; and see Gregg's reply to criticism in Charles Gillette, *A Few Historic Records of the Church in the Diocese of Texas during the Rebellion* (New York, 1865), 32-35.

13. William W. Bennett, *A Narrative of the Great Revival Which Prevailed in the Southern Armies during the Late Civil War between the States of the Federal Union* (1876; Harrisonburg, Va., 1989), 99; also, J. Williams Jones, *Christ in the Camp; or, Religion in Lee's Army* (Richmond, Va., 1888); Herman Norton, "Revivalism in the Confederate Armies," *Civil War History* 6 (1960): 410-24; Stephen V. Ash, *When the Yankees Came: Conflict and Chaos in the Occupied South, 1861-1865* (Chapel Hill, N.C., 1995), 69. For the Episcopal Church's role in the Confederate Army and the revival of 1863 see Joseph

Blount Cheshire, *The Church in the Confederate States: A History of the Protestant Episcopal Church in the Confederate States* (New York, 1912), ch. 3. For soldiers' accounts of the great army revival see G. T. Hodnett to Mary Hodnett, Mar. 29, 1863, in *War Was the Place: A Centennial Collection of Confederate Soldier Letters and Old Oak-bowery, Chambers County, Alabama* (West Point, Ga., 1961), 85–86; Tally Simpson to Mary Simpson, April 10, 1863, and Tally Simpson to A. N. Simpson, May 24, 1863, in Guy R. Everson, Jr., and Edward W. Simpson, eds., *"Far, Far from Home": The Wartime Letters of Dick and Tally Simpson, Third South Carolina Volunteers* (New York, 1994), 213, 233; Rhoda Coleman Ellison, *Bibb County, Alabama: The First Hundred Years, 1818–1918* (University, Ala., 1984), 126; LeGrand James Wilson, *The Confederate Soldier* (Memphis, Tenn., 1973), ch. 22; Basil L. Gildersleeve, *The Creed of the Old South, 1865–1915* (Baltimore, 1915), 13; James I. Robertson, Jr., "Soldiers," in *Encyclopedia of the Confederacy,* ed. Current, 4:1498. For the home front see Wight, "Churches in the Confederacy," ch. 3, and Gardiner H. Shattuck, Jr., *A Shield and Hiding Place: The Religious Life of the Civil War Armies* (Macon, Ga., 1987), 21, 43; Shattuck (ch. 4) credits the religious revivals in the Union army with having had a powerful effect on morale and with stimulating a will to victory.

14. Gary W. Gallagher, ed., *Fighting for the Confederacy: The Personal Recollections of General Edward Porter Alexander* (Chapel Hill, N.C., 1989), 59, also 501–2; William H. Trescot, *Memorial on the Life of J. Johnston Pettigrew, Brig. Gen. of the Confederate States Army* (Charleston, S.C., 1870), 6. During the War, Senator Louis T. Wigfall of Texas and John M. Daniel, editor of the *Richmond Examiner,* among others, ridiculed President Davis for his frequent calls for days of fasting and prayer. See E. Merton Coulter, *The Confederate States of America, 1861–1865* (Baton Rouge, La., 1950), 532.

15. See William Maxey to father, July 26, 1861; Herman Camp to

mother, Aug. 3, 1861; Louis Crawford to Edwin Davis, Feb. 26, 1861; all in Mills Lane, ed., *"Dear Mother: Don't Grieve about Me. If I Get Killed, I'll Only Be Dead"* (Savannah, Ga., 1990), 38, 43, 103. See also A. B. Mulligan to mother and sister, Sept. 20, 1862, in *"My Dear Mother and Sisters": Civil War Letters of Capt. A. B. Mulligan,* ed. Olin Fulmer Hutchinson, Jr. (Spartanburg, S.C., 1992), 45; and Peter S. Carmichael, *Lee's Young Artillerist: William R. J. Pegram* (Charlottesville, Va., 1995), 57–58, 111–12. On the preachers' confidence and caution at the beginning of the War see Willard E. Wight, "The Churches and the Confederate Cause," *Civil War History* 6 (1960): 361–73; on the dogged confidence in victory see Gary W. Gallagher, *The Confederate War* (Cambridge, Mass., 1997), chs. 1, 4; see also George Cary Eggleston, *A Rebel's Recollections* (1874; Baton Rouge, La., 1996).

Some Confederate troops offered prayers with more modest objectives. "Lord," one chap pleaded, "if you ain't with us, don't be against us. Just step aside, and watch the damndest fight you ever likely to see" (quoted in James I. Robertson, Jr., "Soldiers," 4:1498).

Responsible Christian ministers have always tried to prevent the passions of war from spilling over into an arrogant assumption of God's favor. Recall, for example, that Billy Graham, among others, reacted with horror to President Harry Truman's announcement of the dropping of the atomic bomb, pleading that only national repentance would spare the world the catastrophe of an atomic war. Despite his militant anticommunism, Graham warned that God even might use atheistic communists to humble a sinful America. See George M. Marsden, *Reforming Fundamentalism: Fuller Seminary and the New Evangelicalism* (Grand Rapids, Mich., 1987), 92–93.

16. Augustus Baldwin Longstreet, *Fast-Day Sermon, Delivered in the Washington Street Methodist Episcopal Church* (Columbia, S.C., 1861); Ferdinand Jacobs, *A Sermon for the Times* (Marion, Ala., 1861); Lamar, *Discourse;* J. C. Mitchell, *A Sermon Delivered in the*

Government State Church (Mobile, Ala., 1861); Joel W. Tucker, *God Sovereign and Man Free* (Fayetteville, N.C., 1862); John Landing Burrows, *Nationality Insured* (Augusta, Ga., 1864), esp. 6–8; History of the Synod Committee, South Carolina Synod of the Lutheran Church in America, *A History of the Lutheran Church in South Carolina* (Columbia, S.C., 1971), 297.

The general message was neither new nor restricted to military matters. Southerners are being tried, not punished, the Reverend William Bell White Howe told the congregation at St. Philip's Church in December 1861, after a great fire in Charleston (Howe, *Cast Down, but Not Forsaken* [Charleston, S.C., 1861]).

17. William H. Wheelwright, *A Discourse Delivered to the Troops Stationed at Gloucester Point, Virginia* (Richmond, Va., 1862), 12; Alexander Gregg, *A Sermon* (Austin, Tex., 1863); William Norwood, *God and Our Country* (Richmond, Va., 1863), 12; W. Rees, *A Sermon on Divine Providence* (Austin, Tex., 1863), 11; LeRoy M. Lee echoed his fellow Methodist, Rees, in *Our Country—Our Dangers—Our Duty* (Richmond, Va., 1863), 12–18. See also Joel W. Tucker, *The Guilt and Punishment of Extortion* (Fayetteville, N.C., 1862); Joseph Clay Stiles, *National Rectitude the Only True Basis of National Prosperity* (Petersburg, Va., 1863). On the revulsion against "extortion" see Drew Gilpin Faust, *The Creation of Southern Nationalism: Ideology and Identity in the Civil War South* (Baton Rouge, La., 1988), ch. 3; and on the widespread hatred of speculators in North and South see Randall C. Jimerson, *The Private Civil War: Popular Thought during the Sectional Conflict* (Baton Rouge, La., 1988), 210–27.

Louis Ferleger has reminded me that it would be hard to find a war anywhere in which complaints about price-gouging could not be heard. Certainly, price-gouging figured in the Northern jeremiads of countless preachers who called for repentance and warned that the North would lose if it did not end corruption, arrest the decline of religious faith, and rededicate itself as a Christian nation. For a typical illustration see B. M. Morris, *Christian Life and Character of the Civil Institutions of the United States* (Philadelphia, 1864), esp. chs. 1, 26. For blacks, as for white abolitionists, slavery itself defied the will of God, and those who practiced it would meet the fate of all rebels against God's law. To blacks, the early defeats suffered by the Union army signaled God's displeasure with the failure to effect their emancipation.

18. William Stillwell to Mollie Stillwell, Aug. 13, 1863, in Lane, ed., *"Dear Mother,"* 260.

19. Clarke quoted in James W. Silver, *Confederate Morale and Church Propaganda* (New York, 1957), 13; F. Stanley Russell to Annie Russell, Nov. 21, 1863, in Douglas Carroll, ed., *The Letters of F. Stanley Russell: The Movement of Company H Thirteenth Virginia Regiment* (Baltimore, 1963), 41; also Dec. 25, 1863 (p. 103).

20. See Rufas H. Barrier to Mathias Barrier, Nov. 11, 1862, Apr. 20, 1863 (quoted), Mar. 4, 1865; William L. Barrier to Mathias Barrier, Jan. 17, 1863; Daniel M. Moose to Mathias Barrier, Mar. 15, 1863; all in Beverly Barrier Troxler and Billy Dawn Barrier Auciello, eds., *"Dear Father": Confederate Letters Never before Published* (n.p., 1989), 7, 20, 78, 103, 132.

21. See Walter Herron Taylor to Bettie Taylor, Feb. 16, Mar. 5, 1865; Mar. 4, 1863; Feb. 2, 1864; all in R. Lockwood Tower with John S. Belmont, eds., *Lee's Adjutant: The Wartime Letters of Colonel Walter Herron Taylor, 1862–1865* (Columbia, S.C., 1995), 223–24, 230, 51, 113; Sarah Morgan Diary, June 10, 1862, in Charles East, ed., *The Civil War Diary of Sarah Morgan* (Athens, Ga., 1991), 112; Eliza Frances Andrews, Apr. 16, 1865, in *The War-Time Diary of a Georgia Girl, 1864–1865* (New York, 1908), 149; Louis M. DeSaussure Plantation Record, Oct. 23–25, 1861, Southern Historical Collection, University of North Carolina, Chapel Hill; on Jones see Edward Riley Crowther, "Baptist Church," in *Encyclopedia of the Confederacy,* ed. Current, 1:130–31.

On the preachers' efforts to shore up morale see the flagrantly biased but still useful Silver, *Confederate Morale;* more reliable is Charles Reagan Wilson, *Baptized in Blood: The Religion of the Lost Cause, 1865–1920* (Athens, Ga., 1980), 5. On the dogged confidence in a Confederate victory almost to the very end of the War see esp. Gallagher, *Confederate War,* ch. 1. See also the reports of Francis W. Dawson, an Englishman in the Confederate army in Virginia (Dawson to mother, Nov. 25, Dec. 25, 1864, in Dawson, *Reminiscences of Confederate Service, 1861–1865,* ed. Bell I. Wiley [Baton Rouge, La., 1980], 204, 208–10).

22. John S. Palmer to Esther Simon Palmer, July 9, 1862, in Louis P. Towles, ed., *A World Turned Upside Down: The Palmers of South Santee, 1818–1881* (Columbia, S.C., 1996), 330; "Journal of Pauline DeCaradeuc Heyward," Aug. 22, 1863, in M. D. Robertson, ed., *A Confederate Lady Comes of Age* (Columbia, S.C., 1992), 22; Samuel Matthews to Robert Matthews, Nov. 19, 1865, Mississippi Department of Archives and History, Jackson; on Cumming see Richard M. Weaver, *The Southern Tradition at Bay: A History of Postbellum Thought,* ed. George Core and M. E. Bradford (Washington, D.C., 1989), 255–56; Bethell Diary, Aug. 7, 1865, also, Jan. [?], Mar. 29, 1866, Bethell Papers; also, Ellen A. Beatty to Rebecca Simpson, Apr. 22, 1861, in Leah and Rebecca Simpson Papers; Letitia A. Walton to Mary E. Watkins, Aug. 5, 1861, in Joseph Watson Correspondence; Susan Cornwall Diary, Feb. 17, 1863. The Bethell, Simpson, Watson, and Cornwall Papers are in the Southern Historical Collection, University of North Carolina, Chapel Hill.

Charles Reagan Wilson (*Baptized in Blood,* 102) has suggested that the ministers refused to admit that slavery had been the source of God's displeasure and emphasized instead the inadequate response to God's bounty. My quarrel with Wilson concerns his implicit underestimation of the distinction to be made between the continued defense of slavery and the admission that the slaveholders had failed in their duty to the slaves (see below, ch. 3).

23. Cheshire, *Church in the Confederate States,* 3, 116–20; Joseph Ruggles Wilson, *Mutual Relations of Masters and Slaves as Taught in the Bible* (Augusta, Ga., 1861). On the response of the religious press see Wight, "Churches in the Confederacy," ch. 5. In 1865, the Episcopal Church of South Carolina counted about 5,500 adult members, 40 percent of whom were black.

24. Catherine Cooper Hopley, *Life in the South from the Commencement of the War, by a British Subject,* 2 vols. (1863; New York, 1971), 2:46–47; Mary Jones Journal, Jan. 11, 1865, in Myers, ed., *Children of Pride,* 1244; Andrews, Apr. 1, 1865, in *War-Time Diary,* 127.

25. Moore, *God Our Refuge,* 11–12; Meade, *Address,* 14; Stephen Elliott, *Sermon,* 11–12; Stephen Elliott, *God's Presence in the Confederate States* (Savannah, Ga., 1861), 21; Stephen Elliott, *Samson's Riddle,* 2; also, Stephen Elliott, *Address to the Thirty-Ninth Annual Convention of the Protestant Episcopal Church of the Diocese of Georgia* (Savannah, Ga., 1861), 9; Verot, *Tract for the Times.*

26. William A. Clebsch, ed., *Journals of the Episcopal Church in the Confederate States of America* (Austin, Tex., 1962), xiii, pt. 2, p. 44, pt. 3, pp. 10–12; Gregg, *Duties,* 19.

27. I. R. Finley, *The Lord Reigneth* (Richmond, Va., 1863), 18; J. William Flynn, ed., *Complete Works of the Reverend Thomas Smyth, D.D.,* 10 vols. (Columbia, S.C., 1908), 7:701–50, 136–37. Also Ernest Trice Thompson, *Presbyterians in the South,* 3 vols. (Richmond, Va., 1963), 2:84.

28. Sarah E. Watkins to Letitia A. Walton, June 27, 1862, in E. Grey Dimond and Herman Hattaway, eds., *Letters from Forest Place: A Plantation Family's Correspondence, 1846–1881* (Jackson, Miss., 1993), 283; Dolly Lunt Burge, Nov. 8, 1864, in James I. Robertson, Jr., ed., *The Diary of Dolly Lunt Burge* (Athens, Ga., 1962), 98.

29. W. H. Holcombe Diary, Oct. 28, 1855, Southern Historical Collection, University of North Carolina, Chapel Hill; [W. A. Cave], *Two Sermons on the Times, Preached in St. John's Church, Tallahas-*

see (Mobile, Ala., 1861), 12–13; R. C. Saffold to Gov. Pettus, Nov. 3, 1862, in John K. Bettersworth, ed., *Mississippi in the Confederacy: As They Saw It* (Baton Rouge, La., 1961), 101; Lillian Kibler, *Benjamin F. Perry: South Carolina Unionist* (Durham, N.C., 1946), 370.

30. "A Slave Marriage Law," *Southern Presbyterian Review* 16 (1863): 145.

31. In general see Pamela Elwyn Thomas Colbenson, "Millennial Thought among Southern Evangelicals, 1830–1860" (Ph.D. diss., Georgia State University, 1980), 200–201. Also, Benjamin F. Riley, *A Memorial History of the Baptists in Alabama* (Philadelphia, 1923), 291; on the Methodists in Georgia see Harold W. Mann, *Atticus Greene Haygood: Methodist Bishop, Editor, and Educator* (Athens, Ga., 1965), 42–44; M. H. Rice, *American Catholic Opinion in the Slavery Controversy* (New York, 1944), 148 n. 50.

32. Calvin H. Wiley, *Scriptural Views of National Trials* (Greensboro, N.C., 1863). See H. Shelton Smith, *In His Image,* 201 n. 139; Gail Williams O'Brien, *The Legal Fraternity and the Making of a New South Community, 1848–1882* (Athens, Ga., 1986), 188 n. 9 (on his opposition to black troops).

33. Isaac Taylor Tichenor, *Fast Day Sermon* (Montgomery, Ala., 1863), 11–13.

34. George Foster Pierce, "The Word of God a Nation's Life," in *Sermons of Bishop Pierce and Rev. B. M. Palmer* (Milledgeville, Ga., 1863), 14–15; for Turner see Clement Eaton, *A History of the Southern Confederacy* (New York, 1961), 219. Also Wight, "Churches in the Confederacy," ch. 5. Bishop Pierce was doubtless replying to the assertions of Lydia Maria Child, among others, that if the slaves could read the Bible, they would never accept their condition (Child, *An Appeal in Favor of that Class of Americans Called Africans* [Boston, 1833], 108).

35. James A. Lyon et al., "Slavery, and the Duties Growing out of the Relation" (Report to the General Assembly of the Presbyterian

Church), *Southern Presbyterian Review* 16 (July 1863): 1-37. See also Thompson, *Presbyterians in the South,* 3:55-62; and the documents in Bettersworth, ed., *Mississippi in the Confederacy,* 246-47. But, as Lyon said in his report, he believed that slavery "in some form" is the destiny of humanity. Lyon was one of the few strong opponents of secession who kept their pulpits. Most of the others left for the North (Wight, "Churches in the Confederacy," ch. 2). After the War, Lyon supported the efforts of those who insisted upon having racially segregated schools (see J. N. Waddell, *Memorials of Academic Life* [Richmond, Va., 1891], 466-68).

36. Lyon et al., "Slavery." For efforts at reform, some modestly successful, by governors and legislators in other Southern states see Faust, *Creation of Southern Nationalism,* 78.

37. Robert L. Dabney, "Memorial of Lieutenant Colonel John T. Thompson of the Third Virginia Cavalry, C.S.A.," and "True Courage," both in *Discussions,* 3:481, 458.

38. William A. Hall, *The Historic Significance of the Southern Revolution* (Petersburg, Va., 1864); J. W. Tucker, *God's Providence,* 9; Hayne quoted in Charles Roberts Anderson, "Charles Gayarre and Paul Hayne: The Last Literary Cavaliers," in *American Studies in Honor of William Kenneth Boyd,* ed. D. K. Jackson (Durham, N.C., 1940), 232.

39. Sally Kollock quoted in Anne Strudwick Nash, *Ladies in the Making* (Hillsborough, N.C., 1964), 23; Sarah Lois Wadley Private Journal, July 26, 1863, Southern Historical Collection, University of North Carolina, Chapel Hill. For an analysis of women writers' reactions to the defeat see Weaver, *Southern Tradition at Bay,* 254-59, and Sarah Elizabeth Gardner, "'Blood and Irony': Southern Women's Narratives of the Civil War, 1861-1915" (Ph.D. diss., Emory University, 1996), 34-35, 54-55; Edmund Ruffin provided the most famous case of suicide when his beloved South went down. Other planters contemplated suicide in the wake of expropriations by federals and blacks (Ash, *When the Yankees Came,* 212-13).

40. See the viewpoints expressed in 1866 in the Baptist *Christian Index* (Macon, Ga.) and *Religious Herald* (Richmond, Va.); Nannie M. Eiland Lewis to Mary D. Norman, Oct. 7, 1866, in Susan Lott Clark, *Southern Letters and Life in the Mid 1800s* (Waycross, Ga., 1993), 288; Elizabeth Hardin quoted in Gallagher, *Confederate War,* 166; on Cox see Ash, *When the Yankees Came,* 212–13.

41. Carmichael, *Lee's Young Artillerist,* 156–57; David Wesley Martin in Colleen Morse Elliott and Louise Armstrong Moxley, eds., *The Tennessee Civil War Veterans Questionnaires,* 5 vols. (Easley, S.C., 1985), 4:1490; Susan Emeline Jeffreys Caldwell to Lycurgus Washington Caldwell, Jan. 15, 1865, in J. Michael Welton, ed., *"My Heart Is So Rebellious": The Caldwell Letters, 1861–1865* (Warrenton, Va., 1993), 255; William Pitt Chambers, Feb. 15, 1864, Jan. 1, 1865, in Richard A. Baumgartner, ed., *Blood and Sacrifice: The Civil War Journal of a Confederate Soldier* (Huntington, W.Va., 1994), 120, 191. Sarah Morgan's outburst against God passed quickly (Morgan Diary, June 3, 1862, in East, ed., *Civil War Diary,* 104). When it began to dawn on William Porcher DuBose that the Confederacy would lose, it came like a "shock of death," but he kept his faith in God to the end (DuBose, *Turning Points in My Life* [New York, 1912], 49–50).

42. Sarah Woolfolk Wiggins, ed., *The Journals of Josiah Gorgas, 1857–1878* (Tuscaloosa, Ala., 1995), xviii, 197 (July 1, 1866); Wise, *End of an Era,* 37. On the postwar crisis of faith and paralysis of the Baptist churches in the wake of financial stringency and social disruption see Paul Harvey, *Redeeming the South: Religious Cultures and Racial Identities among Southern Baptists, 1865–1925* (Chapel Hill, N.C., 1997), ch. 1.

43. Brown quoted in White, *Southern Presbyterian Leaders,* 347.

44. Louisa C. Hillyer, "The Story of Shaler Granby Hillyer," in *The Life and Times of Judge Junius Hillyer (from His Memoirs)* (Tignall, Ga., 1989), 137; on Gadsden see the tribute from the *Monthly Record,* Aug. 1871, in James H. Elliott, ed., *Tributes to the Memory of the Rev. C. P. Gadsden, with Thirty of His Sermons* (Charleston, S.C.,

1872), 17–18; on Wingate see George Washington Paschal, *History of Wake Forest College,* 3 vols. (Wake Forest, N.C., 1935–43), 1:445.

45. Frances Brokenbrough, *A Mother's Parting Words to Her Soldier Boy* (Petersburg, Va., n.d.), 1–3; Ellen R. House Diary, Dec. 31, 1863; Apr. 23, Dec. 26, 1865; in Daniel E. Sutherland, ed., *A Very Violent Rebel: The Civil War Diary of Ellen Renshaw House* (Knoxville, Tenn., 1996), 75, 162, 198, also 203.

Some preachers, like W. H. Vernor of Lewisburg, Tennessee, and J. W. Tucker of Fayetteville, North Carolina, came close to declaring that the righteousness of the Southern cause, including slavery, guaranteed God's favor and a military victory, but the full context of their sermons suggests that even they may not have meant to give that impression. See, e.g., Vernor, *Sermon,* 11–13; J. W. Tucker, *God's Providence,* 6–7.

46. Willard E. Wight, "Jean-Pierre Augustin Marcellin Verot," in *Dictionary of Georgia Biography,* ed. Kenneth Coleman and Charles Stephen Carr, 2 vols. (Athens, Ga., 1983), 2:1019; Lyon quoted in Thompson, *Presbyterians in the South,* 3:62; for Palmer et al. see editors' note to Adger et al., eds., *Collected Writings,* 4:380; LeGrand James Wilson, *Confederate Soldier,* 210 n. 2.

47. Dagg, *Manual of Theology,* 1:37–38; Robert G. Gardener, "The Alabama Female Athenaeum and John Leadley Dagg in Alabama," *Alabama Baptist Historian* 5 (1969): 21. Baptist publications, like those of other denominations, ruefully acknowledged that God had punished the South for having failed to do full justice to its slaves. The Baptist churches, which had done nothing to discipline masters who broke up slave families, noted officially in 1863 that the South was failing in its duty to protect slave families (Harvey, *Redeeming the South,* 38–39; Grier, "North Carolina Baptists," 14–15).

48. For Atkinson see Cheshire, *Church in the Confederate States,* 131–34; on the women novelists see Gardner, "'Blood and Irony,'" 106–7; for Flournoy see Diane Neale and Thomas W. Krem, *The*

Lion of the South: General Thomas C. Hindman (Macon, Ga., 1993), 210; Arney Robinson Childs, ed., *The Private Journal of Henry William Ravenel, 1859–1887* (Columbia, S.C., 1947), 219, 242–43, 251–52.

Before Atkinson became bishop of North Carolina in 1853, he had been blocked for a bishopric in South Carolina because he was considered critical of slavery. Atkinson, who emancipated his own slaves but opposed the abolitionist agitation, had declined a bishopric in Indiana in the 1840s because he wanted to remain in a slave state and try to alleviate the rigors of slavery (William S. Powell, ed., *Dictionary of North Carolina Biography,* 5 vols. so far [Chapel Hill, N.C., 1979–94], 1:62–63).

49. "The Peace of God" (Mar. 8, 1863) in Thomas E. Peck, *Miscellanies,* ed. Thomas C. Johnson, 3 vols. (Richmond, Va., 1895–97), 2:93. See "The Spirit of Prayer," "The Signs of the Times in the World," "Unbelief in Christ the Greatest of Sins," "The Rest of the People of God," and "The Nature of Prayer," all in John L. Girardeau, *Sermons,* ed. George A. Blackburn (Columbia, S.C., 1907), 268–92, 91–112, 357–68, 333–34, 350, 254, 268–82, 312–20.

Well after the War the Calvinist Girardeau, in a theological treatise that opposed the fatalistic tendencies in supralapsarianism but made no direct mention of the fate of slavery or the Confederacy, wrote, "Nothing comes to pass without his efficient or his permissive ordination; some things come to pass without his predetermination; but he equally knows them all" (Girardeau, *The Will in Its Theological Relations* [Columbia, S.C., 1891], 400; this is the theme of ch. 4).

50. References to Babylon abounded, but for an extended invocation see Pinckney, *Nebuchadnezzar's Fault and Fall.* Some of the preachers seem to have grasped the point that the great theologian Hans Urs von Balthasar made in the twentieth century: The ultimate issue remains "the Babylon within us" (*A Theology of History* [San Francisco, 1994], 150–51).

Chapter Three. In Your Fathers' Stead

1. V. S. Davis, "Stephen Elliott," ch. 8; T. C. Thornton, *An Inquiry into the History of Slavery* (Washington, Miss., 1841), pt. 5.

Antislavery Southerners, some of whom were extreme racists, also argued against the perpetuity of slavery. John Jacobus Flournoy, like the better known Hinton Helper, assailed slavery for protecting blacks from the extermination they deserved, and he ridiculed James H. Hammond for thinking that black slavery was here to stay. See Flournoy to R. F. W. Allston, Dec. 1858, in J. H. Easterby, ed., *The South Carolina Rice Plantation, as Revealed in the Papers of Robert F. W. Allston* (Chicago, 1945), 146. For a particularly sophisticated statement of the argument for the perpetuity of slavery see John Fletcher, *Studies on Slavery, in Easy Lessons* (Natchez, Miss., 1852), esp. 290; for an illustration of a prominent politician who echoed Fletcher see Herbert J. Doherty, *Richard Keith Call, Southern Unionist* (Gainesville, Fla., 1968), 139–41; and for an illustration of the argument on black progress see G. H. Clark, "Sermon in St. John's Church, Nov. 28, 1860," in Jon L. Wakelyn, ed., *Southern Pamphlets on Secession, November 1860–April 1861* (Chapel Hill, N.C., 1996), 55–62. The question of perpetuity was often debated within the context of viewpoints on the millennium; see Colbenson, "Millennial Thought," 190–92.

2. Adger, "Human Rights and Slavery," 569–87; Thornton Stringfellow, "Examination," 520–21; Tise, *Proslavery,* 303. For Miles see Ralph Luker, *A Southern Tradition in Theology and Social Criticism, 1830–1930: The Religious Liberalism and Social Conservatism of James Warley Miles, William Porcher DuBose and Edgar Gardner Murphy* (New York, 1984). Thomas R. R. Cobb slithered on the question of perpetuity, insisting that slavery would last until the final triumph of Christianity (Cobb, *Inquiry,* 63).

3. Furman, "Exposition," 283; Frederick A. Ross, *Slavery Or-*

dained of God (Philadelphia, 1857), 6, 7, 121 ff; Armstrong, *Christian Doctrine of Slavery,* 133 ff; the text of Palmer's sermon is in Thomas Cary Johnson, *The Life and Letters of Benjamin Morgan Palmer* (Richmond, Va., 1906), 206–19; see also Benjamin Morgan Palmer, *A Discourse before the General Assembly of South Carolina on December 10, 1863* (Columbia, S.C., 1864), 14–15; also Thompson, *Presbyterians in the South,* 1:556. For privately expressed views along the same lines see Calvin Taylor to [?], Feb. 6, 1838, in Taylor Papers, Louisiana State University, Baton Rouge; James Henry Greenlee Diary, Dec. 31, 1848, Southern Historical Collection, University of North Carolina, Chapel Hill; Franc M. Carmack Diary, Feb. 1860 ("The Curse of the Sun"), Southern Historical Collection, University of North Carolina, Chapel Hill.

4. Ernst Troeltsch, *The Social Teachings of the Christian Churches,* trans. Olive Wyon, 2 vols. (London, 1950), vol. 1, ch. 1; M. I. Finley, *Ancient Slavery and Modern Ideology* (New York, 1980), 15, 120–21; Paul Tillich, *Systematic Theology,* 3 vols. (Chicago, 1951–63), 3:263. On the influence of Christianity in the transition to freedom in Europe see also David Brion Davis, *The Problem of Slavery in Western Culture* (Ithaca, N.Y., 1966), and Orlando Patterson, *Slavery and Social Death: A Comparative Study* (Cambridge, Mass., 1982).

5. Samuel Seabury, *American Slavery Distinguished from the Slavery of English Theorists and Justified by the Law of Nature* (New York, 1861), 293–94; Thomas Roderick Dew, *A Digest of the Laws, Customs, Manners, and Institutions of the Ancient and Modern Nations* (New York, 1854), 406, 495; Cobb, *Inquiry,* xcvi–xcvii, ch. 2; John Taylor, *An Inquiry into the Principles and Policy of the Government of the United States* (1814; Indianapolis, 1969), 251; Nathaniel Beverley Tucker, *A Series of Lectures on the Science of Government* (Philadelphia, 1845), 301; Samuel Nott, *Slavery and the Remedy; or, Principles and Suggestions for a Remedial Code* (Boston, 1856), 36.

6. Harvey, *Redeeming the South,* ch. 1.

7. Among the prominent orthodox Calvinists, Thornwell, John Adger, Samuel Cassells, W. T. Hamilton, Ferdinand Jacobs, Joseph Stiles, and J. L. Wilson did not mention the curse with reference to blacks, and George Howe emphatically rejected it. Dabney had doubts (see Robert L. Dabney, *Defence of Virginia (and Through Her of the South) in Recent and Pending Contests against the Sectional Party* [1867; New York, 1969], 104). On the secular skeptics see William Kaufman Scarborough, ed., *The Diary of Edmund Ruffin,* 3 vols. (Baton Rouge, La., 1972–89), 1:xxxii, xxvi, xxxi; David Brion Davis, *Problem,* 63–64 n. 2. In general see Thomas Virgil Peterson, *Ham and Japheth: The Mythic World of Whites in the Antebellum South* (Metuchen, N.J., 1978).

8. David Brion Davis, *Slavery and Human Progress* (New York, 1984), 135; Stephen Douglas, Aug. 21, 1858, in Harold Holzer, ed., *The Lincoln-Douglas Debates: The First Complete, Unexpurgated Text* (New York, 1993). See also Paul Johnson, *The Birth of the Modern: World Society, 1815–1830* (London, 1992), 242–44; William Sumner Jenkins, *Pro-Slavery Thought in the Old South* (Gloucester, Mass., 1935), 40; Tise, *Proslavery,* 231; Reginald Horsman, *Josiah Nott of Mobile: Southerner, Physician, and Racial Theorist* (Baton Rouge, La., 1987), 12, 36, 283–84; Weymouth T. Jordan, *Ante-Bellum Alabama: Town and Country* (Tallahassee, Fla., 1957), 97. The monogenesis-polygenesis debate dominated inquiries into race during the eighteenth century. The monogenists stressed the deterioration of certain races from the common origin of the human race. An increasingly popular corollary had weaker races dying out in a protracted struggle for existence (John C. Greene, *The Death of Adam: Evolution and Its Impact on Western Thought* [Ames, Iowa, 1959], chs. 8, 10). The monogenists prevailed during the eighteenth century, but even Lord Kames accepted monogenesis as biblical and placed racial divergence as a consequence of the Tower of Babel.

The polygenists gained strength during the nineteenth century with increasing archeological findings. For the spread of a positive view of polygenesis in the South after the War see Macrae, *Americans at Home,* 307.

9. See "Christian Doctrine of Slavery" and "National Sins," both in Adger et al., eds., *Collected Writings,* 4:402–3, 542–43; also Robert J. Breckinridge, *The Knowledge of God, Objectively Considered as a Science of Positive Truth, Both Inductive and Deductive* (New York, 1858), 23; see also Thompson, *Presbyterians in the South,* 3:25.

10. McTyeire, *Duties,* 136; also Bishop Andrew's "Religious Instruction of the Negroes," written for the *New Orleans Christian Advocate* and republished as an appendix to McTyeire, *Duties,* 219–63.

There is no evidence that masters who accepted or rejected polygenesis treated their slaves differently on that account. Brutes could be found everywhere among those who professed Christian values and rejected scientific arguments, and kind masters could be found among the loudest adherents of polygenesis.

11. James Warley Miles, *The Relation between the Races at the South* (Charleston, S.C., 1861), 15, 18.

12. James Warley Miles, *Philosophic Theology; or, Ultimate Grounds of All Religious Belief in Reason* (Charleston, S.C., 1849), 230–31. Miles did not publicly endorse polygenesis, but he could hardly have made his position clearer (see Luker's admirable *Southern Tradition,* 78–80, esp. 114–15). William Porcher DuBose, Miles's heir in liberal theology, became enamored of Herbert Spencer's evolutionary sociology after the War. On miscegenation as sin see Claude H. Nolen, *The Negro's Image in the South: The Anatomy of White Supremacy* (Lexington, Ky., 1968), ch. 3.

13. David M. Reimers, *White Protestantism and the Negro* (New York, 1965), ch. 2; Nolen, *Negro's Image,* ch. 1; Spain, *At Ease in Zion,* ch. 4. On the use of Noah's curse see J. O. Buswell, III, *Slavery,*

Segregation, and Scripture (Grand Rapids, Mich., 1964), 59, 63–64. Polemicists especially cited Acts 17:26; Cheshire, *Church in the Confederate States,* 106.

14. On the campaign against immorality see Spain, *At Ease in Zion,* ch. 1; Ted Ownby, *Subduing Satan: Religion, Recreation, and Manhood in the Rural South, 1865–1920* (Chapel Hill, N.C., 1990), 8–9.

15. Hoge quoted in Charles Reagan Wilson, *Baptized in Blood,* 22.

16. Before the War the Presbyterians had directly associated the federal doctrine of original sin and the federal polity of their church with the reigning Southern interpretation of the U.S. Constitution and, beyond that, with God-ordained political and social order. Thornwell, known as "the Calhoun of the Church," himself drew attention to the correspondences of Presbyterian doctrine to Southern political theory. See Eugene D. Genovese, *The Slaveholders' Dilemma: Freedom and Progress in Southern Conservative Thought, 1820–1860* (Columbia, S.C., 1991).

17. Samuel Davies Baldwin, *Dominion; or, the Unity and Trinity of the Human Race* (Nashville, Tenn., 1858), 428 ff, 447; Robert L. Dabney, "The World White to the Harvest," in *Discussions,* 1:590–91; "The Sacrifice of Christ," in Adger et al., eds., *Collected Writings,* 2:439–40; Breckinridge quoted in Howard, "Robert J. Breckinridge," 332.

18. William O. Prentiss, *A Sermon Preached at St. Peter's Church, Charleston . . . Nov. 21, 1860* (Charleston, S.C., 1860), 15–16; Pendleton quoted in Ervin L. Jordan, Jr., *Black Confederates and Afro-Yankees in Civil War Virginia* (Charlottesville, Va., 1995), 117. Thornwell, a longtime Unionist who opposed nullification and held out against secession until the eleventh hour, supported annexations to round out the continent at least as early as 1845 (Farmer, *Metaphysical Confederacy,* 246–47).

19. Wightman, *Glory of God,* 7, 9, 13, 14. The slogan "Cotton Is

King" was nonetheless denounced by leading clergymen as a sinful attempt to deny the providence of God (Henry Niles Pierce, *Sermons,* 4-5; George Foster Pierce, "Word of God," 17).

20. Pringle, *Slavery in the Southern States,* 37-38; Sawyer, *Southern Institutes,* 162, 196-97; Fletcher, *Studies on Slavery,* 384; *Jefferson Monument Magazine* 2 (1851): 274; Cobb, *Inquiry,* 106; R. E. C., "The Problem of Free Society," *Southern Literary Messenger* 27 (1858): 93-94; Albert T. Bledsoe, "The Latin Races in America," *Southern Review* 9 (1841): 322-24; James P. Holcombe, "Is Slavery Consistent with Natural Law?" (Address to State Agricultural Society at the Agricultural Fair in Petersburg, Nov. 4, 1858), *Southern Literary Messenger* 27 (1858): 405; also John C. Calhoun, *A Disquisition on Government and Selections from the Discourse* (Indianapolis, 1953), 47-48.

21. Whitaker, *History of the Protestant Episcopal Church,* 202-3.

22. Maria Genoino Caravaglios, *The American Catholic Church and the Negro Problem in the XVIII-XIX Centuries,* trans. Ernest L. Unterkoefler (Charleston, S.C., 1974), 203; Robert L. Dabney, *Systematic Theology* (2d ed., 1878; Carlisle, Pa., 1985), 292-93.

23. Thomas C. Johnson, ed., *Life and Letters of Robert Lewis Dabney,* 396-97; on Dabney's lurid images see Charles Reagan Wilson, *Baptized in Blood,* 106-7. On Palmer see Thomas C. Johnson, *Life and Letters of Benjamin Morgan Palmer,* 472-73; and Daniel G. Reid et al., eds., *Dictionary of Christianity in America* (Downer's Grove, Ill., 1990), 860. Randle quoted in Mann, *Atticus Greene Haygood,* 196. On resistance to scientific racism see Girardeau, *Will,* 31-32; Adger et al., eds., *Collected Writings,* 2:64; Charles Hodge, *Systematic Theology,* 3 vols. (1871; Grand Rapids, Mich., 1993), vol. 2, ch. 4; Jaroslav Pelikan, *The Christian Tradition: A History of the Development of Doctrine,* 5 vols. (Chicago, 1989), 5:206, 209, 256.

24. George G. Smith, *A History of Georgia Methodism from 1786 to 1866* (Atlanta, 1913), 333-34. After the War, laity blocked the bishop's efforts to promote racial integration in the Episcopal Church of

South Carolina: see Lyon G. Tyler, "Drawing the Color Line in the Episcopal Diocese of South Carolina, 1876–1890: The Role of Edward McCrady, Father and Son," *South Carolina Historical Magazine* 91 (1990): 107–24.

25. As Ronald G. Walters remarks in his superb study of abolitionism, "Attitudes that helped men and women respond to the evils of slavery finally blended into Darwinism and laissez-faire economics, which were to serve as props for late nineteenth-century racism" (Walters, *The Antislavery Appeal: American Abolitionism after 1830* [Baltimore, 1976], xvi–xvii).

26. See David L. Chappell, *Mind of the Segregationist* (forthcoming).

27. Alan Davies, *Infected Christianity: A Study of Modern Racism* (Kingston, Ont., 1988), esp. ch. 5.

Chapter Four. An Uncertain Trumpet

1. *Richmond Religious Herald,* Oct. 19, 1865; for the text of the Methodist pastoral letter see Shipp, *History of Methodism,* 498–512; Thomas E. Peck, "The Judicial Law of Moses," in *Miscellanies,* ed. Thomas C. Johnson, 157–66.

2. J. Henry Smith, *A Sermon Delivered at Greensboro, N.C., on the 5th of December, 1861* (Greensboro, N.C., 1862), 11; James Henley Thornwell to Nancy Thornwell, Apr. 12, 1862, Presbyterian Historical Association, Montreat, N.C.

3. Landrum, *Battle Is God's;* Nicholas Hamner, *The Doubting Christian Encouraged* (Uniontown, Ala., 1864); Wilmer, *Future Good;* I. R. Finley, *Lord Reigneth;* David Seth Doggett, *The War and Its Close* (Richmond, Va., 1864). For continued emphases on ultimate victory see W. T. D. Dalzell, *Thanksgiving to God: A Sermon* (San Antonio, Tex., 1863); Higgins, *Mountain Moved.* And see Snay, *Gospel of Disunion,* esp. ch. 5.

4. Robert L. Dabney to Moses Drury Hoge, Aug. 16, 1865, in

Thomas Cary Johnson, ed., *Life and Letters of Robert Lewis Dabney,*
304–7, quotation on 305; for Dabney's speech at Davidson see *The
Land We Love* 5 (Sept. 1868): 444. Girardeau, *Sermons,* 91–112; Andrews, July 27, 1865, in *War-Time Diary,* 351. For examples from
early Reconstruction see Jack Maddex, "Postslavery Millennialism:
Social Eschatology in Antebellum Southern Calvinism," *American
Quarterly* 31 (1979): 46–68. In the 1870s Dabney kept returning
to the theme that God's chastisements must be accepted as signs
of his benevolence and concern to save souls (*Systematic Theology,*
557, 818).

In January 1865, Edmund Ruffin was hardly alone in seeing in the
destruction of slavery not only "a wound to our economical interests," but also an injury to "refinement of manners, & civilization,
which would not be cured & recovered from in a century" (Scarborough, ed., *Diary,* 3:712).

5. Benjamin Morgan Palmer, *The Life and Letters of James Hen-
ley Thornwell, D.D., LL.D.* (Richmond, Va., 1875), 482–83; Mary
Chesnut Diary, Sept. 12, 1864, in Woodward, ed., *Mary Chesnut's
Civil War,* 644.

6. For an elaboration of my interpretation of Thornwell and, by
extension, the others see Genovese, *Slaveholders' Dilemma,* ch. 2.
On Thornwell see also William W. Freehling, *The Reintegration
of American History: Slavery and the Civil War* (New York, 1994),
ch. 4; Farmer, *Metaphysical Confederacy,* esp. ch. 7.

7. Henry Hughes, *Treatise on Sociology, Theoretical and Practical* (1854; New York, 1968), esp. 113, 149, 154, 216–17; and see the
splendid analysis of Hughes's thought in Douglas Ambrose, *Henry
Hughes and Proslavery Thought in the Old South* (Baton Rouge, La.,
1996), esp. ch. 3. Holcombe, "Is Slavery Consistent with Natural
Law?" 418.

8. John Greenleaf Whittier, *Justice and Expediency; or, Slavery
Considered with a View to Its Rightful and Effectual Remedy, Abolition* (Haverhill, N.H., 1833), 5; William Goodell, *The American Slave*

Code in Theory and Practice (1853; New York, 1969), 75–76. In the 1830s, opponents of slavery, sliding between gradual and immediate emancipation, advanced various proposals for systems that would resemble *métayage* (see, e.g., Robert H. Rose to James Gillespie Birney, Dec. 20, 1834, July 15, 1836, in Dumond, ed., *Letters*, 1:159–60, 336–42). When these proposals came from the antislavery side, they generally implied an eventual transition to a free-labor system.

9. The text of Carlyle to Tucker, Oct. 31, 1851, may be found in Mrs. George P. Coleman, ed., *Virginia Silhouettes: Contemporary Letters Concerning Negro Slavery in the State of Virginia* (Richmond, Va., 1934), 46–49, quotation on 48. Carlyle doubtless knew, as some Southerners did, that the ancient Israelites and the peoples who lived under the Code of Hammurabi acknowledged a slave's right to a peculium. Tucker had himself suggested the need for reform, but, caught up in the sectional struggle over the Compromise of 1850, he did not enjoy Carlyle's response.

10. Benjamin to Porcher, Dec. 21, 1864, as quoted in E. N. Evans, *Judah P. Benjamin: The Jewish Confederate* (New York, 1988), 278; also 281–89. Benjamin, among many others, undoubtedly knew how attached the slaves were to the land and how readily they saw it as their own. See, e.g., Charles Joyner, *Down by the Riverside: A South Carolina Slave Community* (Urbana, Ill., 1984), 42–43, 129.

11. *Henderson v. Vaulx,* in Catterall, ed., *Judicial Cases,* vol. 2, pt. 2, 504–5.

12. *Alabama House of Representatives Journal,* 1857–58 sess., 28; Thomas D. Morris, *Southern Slavery and the Law,* 97; Henry G. Connor, *John Archibald Campbell: Associate Justice of the United States Supreme Court, 1853–1861* (Boston, 1920), 105–7; Tony Fryer, "Law and the Antebellum Southern Economy: An Interpretation," in *Ambivalent Legacy: A Legal History of the South,* ed. David J. Bodenhamer and James W. Ely, Jr. (Jackson, Miss., 1984), 61–62.

13. Samuel Walker Diary, July 27, 1857, Tulane University; Frederick Bancroft, *Slave Trading in the Old South* (New York, 1959),

200 n. 6. Strikingly, the Lyon report made no mention of binding slaves to the soil. But then, its Presbyterian authors were well read in political economy.

14. "Carey on the Slave Trade," in McCord, *Political and Social Essays,* 408–9; first published in *Southern Quarterly Review* 25 (1854): 170–71. See also Eugene D. Genovese and Elizabeth Fox-Genovese, "Slavery, Economic Development, and the Law: The Dilemma of Southern Political Economists, 1800–1860," *Washington and Lee Law Review* 41 (1984): 26. And on the deep commitment of white Southerners to the notion that emancipation would condemn the blacks to virtual genocide see Eugene D. Genovese, "'The Negroes' Best and Only Friend': The Slaveholders' Argument on Black Incapacity to Compete in the Capitalist Marketplace," in Valeria Gennaro Lerda, ed., *Le stelle e le strisce: studi americani e militare in onore di Raimondo Luraghi,* 2 vols. (Milano, 1998), 1:143–62.

15. "Slave Marriage Law," 145, 147 (quoted).

16. The importance of the rights of serfs in the development of Western law is emphasized in Harold J. Berman, *Law and Revolution: The Formation of the Western Legal Tradition* (Cambridge, Mass., 1983), 10, 320–22, 337.

17. Albert Barnes, *An Inquiry into the Scriptural Views of Slavery* (Philadelphia, 1857), 13, 135; Rufus W. Clark, *A Review of the Rev. Moses Stuart's Pamphlet on Slavery, Entitled Conscience and Constitution* (Boston, 1850), 19, 30 (quoted).

18. George F. Simmons, *Two Sermons on the Kind Treatment and on the Emancipation of Slaves* (Boston, 1840), quotations on 20–23, 27.

19. O'Neall quoted in A. E. Keir Nash, "Negro Rights," 16; see also 182–83. Nash's fine essay, which admirably reviews and comments upon O'Neall's work as a reformer, is marred by his erroneous attribution of antislavery sentiments to O'Neall and, indeed, to most Unionists.

20. For an elaboration of the property question see Elizabeth Fox-

Genovese and Eugene D. Genovese, *Fruits of Merchant Capital: Slavery and Bourgeois Property in the Rise and Expansion of Capitalism* (New York, 1983). For the difficulties of meshing bourgeois law with the exigencies of modern slave society see Mark V. Tushnet, *The American Law of Slavery: Considerations of Humanity and Interest* (Princeton, N.J., 1981).

21. For some clerical attacks on the doctrine of property in man see Charles Colcock Jones, *Religious Instruction;* Messmer, ed., *Works of John of England,* 5:187, 194; Samuel I. Cassells, *Servitude and the Duty of Masters to Their Servants* (Norfolk, Va., 1843), 5; Fuller and Wayland, *Domestic Slavery,* 9, 23, 140–41, 143, and Fuller's Letter 3; H. B. Bascom, *Sermons from the Pulpit* (Louisville, Ky., 1850), 247; Adger et al., eds., *Collected Writings,* 4:409–12; Dabney, *Defence,* 94; Adger, "Human Rights and Slavery," 579–82; W. P. Harrison, *The Gospel among the Slaves* (Nashville, Tenn., 1893), 39; Jacobs, *Committing of Our Cause,* 69n. Thornwell's views are ably discussed in Mitchell Snay, "American Thought and Southern Distinctiveness: The Southern Clergy and the Sanctification of Slavery," *Civil War History* 35 (1989): 316–19.

For secular versions see Cobb, *Inquiry,* esp. 83, 103–4; Sawyer, *Southern Institutes,* 219–20, 312–14; [A North Carolinian], *Slavery Considered,* 21; E. A Pollard, *A Southern History of the War,* 2 vols. in 1 (1866; Richmond, Va., 1977), 2:202n; Stephens, *Constitutional View,* 1:539–40; 2:25.

22. Robert L. Dabney, "Principles of Christian Economy," in *Discussions,* 1:132; John Donald Wade, *Augustus Baldwin Longstreet: A Study of the Development of Culture in the South* (New York, 1924), 138.

23. James Johnston Pettigrew, *Notes on Spain and the Spaniards in the Summer of 1859, with a Glance at Sardinia. By a Carolinian* (Charleston, S.C., 1861), 7, 15, 16, 378, 381; Elliott, quoted in Robert Nichols Olsberg, "A Government of Class and Race": William H.

Trescot and the South Carolina Chivalry, 1860–1865 (Ph.D. diss., University of South Carolina, 1972), 109 n. 39; John Berrien Lindsley, "Table Talk," June 2, 1862, in Lindsley Papers, Tennessee State Library and Archives, Nashville; also Scarborough, ed., *Diary*, 1: 163, 3:59; William A. Smith, *Lectures on the Philosophy and Practice of Slavery* (Nashville, Tenn., 1856), 267; Colbenson, "Millennial Thought," 70–75.

Epilogue. The Sixth Seal

1. Thomas L. Stokes, *The Savannah* (1951; Athens, Ga., 1979), 9.

2. Mason in James Madison, *Notes of Debates in the Federal Convention of 1787* (Athens, Ohio, 1966), 504.

3. Spencer B. King, Jr., *Darien: The Death and Rebirth of a Southern Town* (Macon, Ga., 1981), 6–7 (petition quoted); on the burning of Darien see ch. 6. This short, eloquent book tells the story of Darien well and deserves to be much better known and more widely read. Those who saw the film *Glory* will recall its depiction of the burning of Darien.

Index